FORTY
HADEETH
FOR MUSLIM YOUTH
AND BEGINNERS

AN EASY INTRODUCTION
TO THE STUDY OF
THE PROPHET'S
NARRATIONS

صلى الله عليه وسلم

MAY ALLAH RAISE HIS RANK
AND GRANT HIM PEACE

MOOSAA RICHARDSON & DR. ABDIMALIK MAOW

**First Print (Paperback) Edition:
Safar 1444 (September 2022)**

Richardson, Moosaa.

Maow, Abdimalik.

Forty Hadeeth for Muslim Youth and Beginners, An Easy Introduction to the Study of the Prophet's Narrations / Author: Moosaa Richardson & Dr. Abdimalik Maow.

ISBN 979-8844351082

1. Nonfiction —Religion —Islam —General.

2. Nonfiction —Religion —Islam —Sunni.

TABLE OF CONTENTS

FOREWORD

All praise is due to Allah, the Lord, Creator, and Sustainer of the entire creation. May He raise the rank of the best of His prophets and messengers, our Prophet Muhammad, and all of his family, followers, and companions, and may He grant them all peace.

To proceed: This book is a humble effort by two concerned educators to present a small collection of very brief, yet highly impactful, Hadeeth narrations to beginners and young learners. These 43 narrations have been carefully selected from the thousands of narrations found in the two authentic compilations, *Saheeh al-Bukhari* and *Saheeh Muslim*. Five basic points of explanation are included with each Hadeeth to highlight some of the most important benefits that should not be overlooked.

Dr. Abdimalik Maow of Bradford (may Allah bless and reward him) approached me with the first version of this compilation over a year ago. His vision was to prepare an easy and practical study of Hadeeth for young learners, something easier to understand and memorize than the 40 Hadeeth of al-Hafidh an-Nawawi (may Allah have Mercy on him). After many meetings and revisions, we produced a draft which was beta-tested by a number of parents and teachers in the US and UK. After evaluating all the helpful feedback and improving our work, by Allah's Permission, we have arrived at what you have in your hands. We ask Allah to bless it and make it a great benefit for us and for all who study it.

I feel this collection is an important first step for anyone who wishes to study Hadeeth. Let me explain why I believe this book serves as an important precursor to an-Nawawi's classic 40 Hadeeth collection, especially for beginners and young learners, as it relates to three important considerations: the scope, the wordings, and the sources of the narrations.

The first reason why this collection should be studied before an-Nawawi's 40 Hadeeth is its scope. An-Nawawi's narrations are meant to be packed with foundations and principles, covering much of the religion with each narration. Some of those meanings are quite complex and require detailed explanations. Consider how the Hadeeth of Jibreel, for example, an-Nawawi's second narration, covers the entire religion, from the pillars of Islam, to the tenets of creed, to signs of the Day of Judgment, and many other detailed matters, which cannot be actualized without great efforts and dedication in many sittings. In fact, in the year 1436 (2015), I taught this single narration in a total of 29 weekly classes, using a relatively brief explanation! This collection, on the other hand, is meant to be simple and basic. Reading any one of these narrations with its five points of benefit with a small group of youth or beginners could be done in a single sitting of just a few minutes.

Additionally, the wordings of this collection of Hadeeth are generally very brief and easy to understand and memorize. Consider the difficulty of explaining to beginners, **"When a slave-girl gives birth to her master,"** from an-Nawawi's second narration, or the prohibition of artificial bids at an auction, the **"Najsh"** operation, among the many forbidden dealings in Hadeeth #35. Compare that to the ease of explaining how Allah considers our hearts and actions, instead of our appearances, in the second narration of this collection, or how our Hadeeth #35 simply invites the learner to appreciate how important good health and free time are.

Furthermore, the advantage of limiting the narrations to the two *Saheeh* compilations of al-Bukhari and Muslim is more suitable for young learners and beginners. This creates a "safe zone" and ensures the authenticity of the narrations, essentially delaying any need to introduce matters connected to the intricate nature of the authentication process employed by Hadeeth scholars. This facilitates the ability to focus on the primary goal of this collection: the basic meanings and how to implement them. Comparatively, imagine explaining to your child or young student what an-Nawawi (may Allah have Mercy on him) said about his 32nd narration:

> It is a *hasan* (sound) narration, collected by Ibn Majah, ad-Daraqutni, and others, with connected chains of transmission. It was also collected by Malik in *al-Mawatta'* in *mursal* form (with a broken chain), from the report of 'Amr ibn Yahya, from his father, from the Prophet (may Allah raise his rank and grant him peace), omitting Abu Sa'eed. It has other routes of transmission which strengthen each other as well.

Of course, the status of that collection, an-Nawawi's 40 Hadeeth, remains exceptional, based on the great heritage of scholarly attention given to it over the centuries. However, for beginners and young learners, we hope it is clear how this collection can be a much easier introduction to the study of Hadeeth, and Allah knows best.

Another subtle feature of this book is the connection which is both intended and commonly referenced between one narration and the next. Whenever possible, we tried to use the last point (Point #5) of each list of benefits to connect the learner to the next Hadeeth. Additionally, the first point typically connects back to the previous narration. With this in place, a Hadeeth study in this book is typically a review of the previous one, as well as a springboard into the topic of the next one, by Allah's Permission.

In the back of this book, the reader will also find two complete texts of the Hadeeth collection, one in Arabic, and the other in English. The Arabic version begins on page 122, and, of course, it reads from right to left. The English version begins on page 108. Recordings of each Hadeeth are also freely available for listening and/or downloading on our masjid's Spreaker channel:

www.spreaker.com/show/40-easy-hadeeth

Additionally, we are in the process of publishing a workbook to accompany this collection, *in shaa' Allah*, which provides educators with excellent resources for their learners in a traditional classroom setting. Engaging activities aid the students in understanding the narrations and how to apply them practically, in pages set up for both classwork and homework. Our vision for a children's course in an Islamic school or homeschool setting includes two full semesters of a weekly Hadeeth class. A teacher's manual will include answer keys to quizzes, practical tips for instruction and class management, as well as exams and additional activities, *in shaa' Allah*. May Allah facilitate its completion and make it a valuable contribution to Islamic school materials.

I would like to thank my beloved brother, my co-author, Dr. Abdimalik Maow (may Allah bless him), for his tremendous initiative, and for all of his important work and follow-up on this project, from start to finish. On his behalf, I would also like to thank all our beloved brothers and sisters who aided us in producing this work, those who were involved in the beta testing, as well as those who reviewed drafts and provided helpful feedback. Especially, we would like to thank the noble brothers, Gibril Harding (USA), Abdul-Muhaymin ibn James (USA), Talhah Mahmood (UK), Ibrahim al-Baljiki (UK), and Qaudir Lalloo (AUS) for their valuable input. May Allah reward them generously.

Lastly, on behalf of my respected co-author, Dr. Abdimalik Maow (may Allah bless him), we invite educators to support us by sharing their insight and experience using these materials. We welcome any corrections, suggestions, or advice that might help make this work better. We view our work as deficient and in need of improvement, so may Allah reward you! May Allah raise the rank of our Prophet Muhammad and grant him and his family and companions an abundance of peace.

Moosaa Richardson

Email: education@firstmuslimmosque.com
Twitter: @1MMeducation

INTRODUCTION

All praise is due to Allah. We praise Him, seek His Assistance, and ask Him to forgive us. We seek refuge with Him from the evils of our own souls and from the bad consequences of our wrongdoings. I testify openly that no one deserves any worship other than Allah, alone without any partner. I further testify that Muhammad was His servant and Messenger (may Allah raise his rank and grant him peace).

To proceed: We have compiled this work to help Muslims memorize short and easy Hadeeth narrations from our Prophet (may Allah raise his rank and grant him peace). This can be used for children from a young age, new Muslims, or any Muslim who likes to learn about the Hadeeth narrations of his Prophet (may Allah raise his rank and grant him peace). Even non-Muslims can use it to get a better idea about the teachings of the Prophet Muhammad (may Allah raise his rank and grant him peace).

Apart from memorization, a very important goal for this work is that people **apply** the teachings of the Prophet (may Allah raise his rank and grant him peace) in their daily lives. A person who struggles to memorize the narrations, but applies well what he has learned, may be much better in the sight of Allah than the one who has memorized all the narrations, but is not so devout in applying them.

To help Muslims to know how to apply the narrations, each Hadeeth has five numbered points included, in order to clarify some of its basic meanings. A person can, for example, take a few minutes in a specified day of the week to go through the narrations with his/her children or study circle and discuss how to apply it in their specific situation(s). One could also individually go through the Hadeeth narrations and contemplate about what he should change in his life, to be included in those who acted upon these words.

Think about Imam Ahmad (may Allah have Mercy on him), a man who had applied every single narration that he had come across, except for a single Hadeeth that he was not able to apply! Also, think about how big his primary Hadeeth collection, the *Musnad*, was! (40,000 narrations!) Are we then not able to exert ourselves to apply this much smaller number of narrations in our lives?

I would like to thank Allah, who has enabled us to set up this work and publish it. Then, I would like to thank our beloved teacher,

Moosaa Richardson, for having good thoughts of me and working together to compile this, as well as all those who have been involved, aiding us to improve this work.

May Allah make this work sincerely for His sake and a means by which the Sunnah of our noble Prophet (may Allah raise his rank and grant him peace) is preserved, held in high regard, and applied throughout the world.

Abdimalik Maow

Email: amaow@hotmail.com
Twitter: @AbdimalikMaow

PART ONE

SINCERITY

& FOLLOWING

الْبَابُ الْأَوَّلُ

الْإِخْلَاصُ وَالْمُتَابَعَةُ

HADEETH 1
Intentions

'Umar (may Allah be pleased with him) reported that the Messenger of Allah (may Allah raise his rank and grant him peace) said:

"Actions are only by the intentions, and every person will only get what he intended."

It was collected by al-Bukhari (1) and Muslim (1907).

<u>**POINTS OF BENEFIT FROM THIS HADEETH:**</u>

1. *Intentions are what a person wants from the action he does.*

2. *Good intentions are for the sake of Allah alone.*

3. *We must seek the pleasure of Allah, His reward, and safety from His Anger and punishment.*

4. *Whoever intends to please Allah with good actions, Allah accepts his actions and rewards him for them.*

5. *The intention of the heart is a very big issue; it connects to all the lessons coming in this book.*

الحديث الأول
النيات

عَنْ عُمَرَ ـرَضِيَ اللهُ عَنْهُ ـ قَالَ: قَالَ رَسُولُ اللهِ ـصَلَّى اللهُ عَلَيْهِ وَسَلَّمَ ـ :

«إِنَّمَا الْأَعْمَالُ بِالنِّيَّاتِ، وَإِنَّمَا لِكُلِّ امْرِئٍ مَا نَوَى.»

أَخْرَجَهُ الْبُخَارِيُّ (١) وَمُسْلِمٌ (١٩٠٧).

ما يستفاد من الحديث:

١ ـ النية هي ما يقصده الشخص من عمله.

٢ ـ النية الحسنة هي ما كان لله وحده.

٣ ـ يجب علينا أن نطلب بأعمالنا رضا الله وثوابه والسلامة من سخطه وعقابه.

٤ ـ من أراد أن يرضي الله بعمله الحسن فالله يتقبل منه ويجزيه خيرا.

٥ ـ نية القلب مسألة عظيمة تدخل في جميع الدروس الآتية في هذا الكتاب.

HADEETH 2
Hearts & Actions

Abu Hurayrah (may Allah be pleased with him) reported that the Messenger of Allah (may Allah raise his rank and grant him peace) said:

"Allah does not look at your shapes or your wealth; instead He looks at your hearts and your actions."

It was collected by Muslim (2564).

POINTS OF BENEFIT FROM THIS HADEETH:

1. *Outward actions are based on inward intentions.*

2. *Appearances and wealth are not important to Allah.*

3. *Hearts and actions are important to Allah.*

4. *We must review our actions and correct them.*

5. *We must review our intentions and correct our hearts.*

الحديث الثاني
القلوب والأعمال

عَنْ أَبِي هُرَيْرَةَ ـرَضِيَ اللهُ عَنْهُ ـ قَالَ: قَالَ رَسُولُ اللهِ ـصَلَّى اللهُ عَلَيْهِ وَسَلَّمَ ـ:

«إنَّ اللهَ لَا يَنْظُرُ إِلَى صُوَرِكُمْ وَأَمْوَالِكُمْ، وَلَكِنْ يَنْظُرُ إِلَى قُلُوبِكُمْ وَأَعْمَالِكُمْ.»

أَخْرَجَهُ مُسْلِمٌ (٢٥٦٤).

ما يستفاد من الحديث:

١ _ الأعمال الظاهرة بالنيات الباطنة.

٢ _ ليس المهم عند الله: الشكل والمال.

٣ _ المهم عند الله: القلب والعمل.

٤ _ يجب علينا أن نراجع أعمالنا ونصلحها.

٥ _ يجب علينا أن نراجع نياتنا ونصلح قلوبنا.

HADEETH 3
Praying For Our Hearts

'Abdullah ibn 'Amr (may Allah be pleased with him) reported that the Messenger of Allah (may Allah raise his rank and grant him peace) said:

"O Allah, Turner of the Hearts! Turn our hearts towards Your obedience!"

It was collected by Muslim (2654).

<u>POINTS OF BENEFIT FROM THIS HADEETH:</u>

1. *Praying for our hearts is the best way to fix them.*

2. *Allah is the only One who turns people's hearts.*

3. *The Messenger (may Allah raise his rank and grant him peace) had the cleanest heart, and he would call upon Allah with this prayer.*

4. *A true believer calls upon Allah to guide his heart all the time.*

5. *A good heart leads a person to obey Allah and His Messenger (may Allah raise his rank and grant him peace).*

الحديث الثالث
إصلاح القلب بالدعاء

عَنْ عَبْدِاللهِ بْنِ عَمْرٍو ـرَضِيَ اللهُ عَنْهُمَاـ قَالَ: قَالَ رَسُولُ اللهِ ـصَلَّى اللهُ عَلَيْهِ وَسَلَّمَـ :

«اللَّهُمَّ مُصَرِّفَ الْقُلُوبِ! صَرِّفْ قُلُوْبَنَا عَلَى طَاعَتِكَ!»

أَخْرَجَهُ مُسْلِمٌ (٢٦٥٤).

ما يستفاد من الحديث:

١ _ الدعاء أفضل وسيلة لإصلاح قلوبنا.

٢ _ الله هو الذي يوجه قلوب الناس.

٣ _ الرسول صلى الله عليه وسلم أطهر الناس قلبا، وهو يدعو الله بهذا الدعاء.

٤ _ المؤمن يدعو الله أن يهدي قلبه دائما .

٥ _ القلب الصالح يهدي صاحبه إلى طاعة الله ورسوله صلى الله عليه وسلم.

HADEETH 4
Obeying the Messenger

Abu Hurayrah (may Allah be pleased with him) reported that the Messenger of Allah (may Allah raise his rank and grant him peace) said:

"Stay away from all things I have forbidden you from; do as much as you can of what I have told you to do."

It was collected by al-Bukhari (7288) and Muslim (1337).

POINTS OF BENEFIT FROM THIS HADEETH:

1. *Good deeds are avoiding forbidden things and doing what we are told to do, with good intentions.*

2. *A true believer stays away from what Allah and His Messenger (may Allah raise his rank and grant him peace) forbid him from.*

3. *A true believer does what Allah and His Messenger have commanded (may Allah raise his rank and grant him peace).*

4. *Doing what we are told is based on our ability, and some people can do more things than others.*

5. *Islam is easy. (Look ahead to Hadeeth 7).*

الحديث الرابع
طاعة الرسول

عَنْ أَبِي هُرَيْرَةَ ـرَضِيَ اللهُ عَنْهُ ـ قَالَ: قَالَ رَسُولُ اللهِ ـصَلَّى اللهُ عَلَيْهِ وَسَلَّمَـ:

«مَا نَهَيْتُكُمْ عَنْهُ فَاجْتَنِبُوهُ، وَمَا أَمَرْتُكُمْ بِهِ فَافْعَلُوا مِنْهُ مَا اسْتَطَعْتُمْ.»

أَخْرَجَهُ الْبُخَارِيُّ (٧٢٨٨) وَمُسْلِمٌ (١٣٣٧)، وَاللَّفْظُ لَهُ.

ما يستفاد من الحديث:

١_ العمل الصالح ترك المنهي عنه وفعل المأمور به بنية حسنة.

٢_ المؤمن يترك ما نهى الله عنه ورسوله صلى الله عليه وسلم.

٣_ المؤمن يفعل ما أمره الله ورسوله صلى الله عليه وسلم.

٤_ المأمور به حسب القدرة، وتختلف القدرة من شخص إلى آخر.

٥_ الدين الإسلامي يسر. [انظر حـ٧]ـ.

HADEETH 5
Towheed

Mu'adh ibn Jabal (may Allah be pleased with him) reported that the Messenger of Allah (may Allah raise his rank and grant him peace) said:

"Allah's right over His servants is that they worship Him alone, without worshipping any partners along with Him."

It was collected by al-Bukhari (5967) and Muslim (30).

POINTS OF BENEFIT FROM THIS HADEETH:

1. *The greatest command in Islam is **towheed**, to worship Allah alone.*

2. *The greatest sin is **shirk**, to direct any act of worship to someone other than Allah.*

3. ***Towheed** was the basic message of all prophets.*

4. *Whoever directs any act of worship to someone other than Allah goes to Hell.*

5. *Whoever worships Allah alone and does not set up any partners with Him goes to Paradise.*

الحديث الخامس
التوحيد

عَنْ مُعَاذِ بْنِ جَبَلٍ _رَضِيَ اللهُ عَنْهُ_، قَالَ: قَالَ رَسُولُ اللهِ _صَلَّى اللهُ عَلَيْهِ وَسَلَّمَ_ :

«حَقُّ اللهِ عَلَى عِبَادِهِ أَنْ يَعْبُدُوهُ وَلاَ يُشْرِكُوا بِهِ شَيْئًا».

أَخْرَجَهُ الْبُخَارِيُّ (٥٩٦٧) وَمُسْلِمٌ (٣٠).

ما يستفاد من الحديث:

١_ هذا الأمر الأعظم في دين الله: التوحيد، وهو عبادة الله وحده.

٢_ ومعه النهي عن الذنب الأعظم: الشرك، وهو صرف شيء من العبادة لغير الله.

٣_ هذا التوحيد هو أصل رسالة جميع الأنبياء.

٤_ من صرف شيئا من العبادة لغير الله دخل النار.

٥_ من عبد الله وحده ولم يشرك به شيئا دخل الجنة.

HADEETH 6
Making Things Easy

Anas (may Allah be pleased with him) reported that the Messenger of Allah (may Allah raise his rank and grant him peace) said:

"Make things easy [for people], and do not make things hard; give good news, and do not run [them] away."

It was collected by al-Bukhari (69) and Muslim (1734).

POINTS OF BENEFIT FROM THIS HADEETH:

1. *Making things easy for people means to help them worship Allah alone, and to help them in other good things.*

2. *Making things hard on people means to add difficulties and to stop them from doing good things.*

3. *Giving good news includes using good words, being positive, and having good manners.*

4. *Running people away includes using bad words, being negative, and having bad manners.*

5. *These are important manners which the Messenger of Allah commanded us to have (may Allah raise his rank and grant him peace).*

الحديث السادس
التيسير

عَنْ أَنَسٍ ـرَضِيَ اللهُ عَنْهُ ـ قَالَ: قَالَ رَسُولُ اللهِ ـصَلَّى اللهُ عَلَيْهِ وَسَلَّمَ ـ :

«يَسِّرُوا وَلاَ تُعَسِّرُوا، وَبَشِّرُوا وَلاَ تُنَفِّرُوا.»

أَخْرَجَهُ الْبُخَارِيُّ (٦٩) وَمُسْلِمٌ (١٧٣٤).

ما يستفاد من الحديث:

١_ التيسير أن تساعد الآخرين على عبادة الله وحده وعلى الخير عموما.

٢_ التعسير أن تشق على الآخرين وتمنعهم من الخير.

٣_ من التبشير استعمال الألفاظ الحسنة والتفاؤل وحسن الخلق.

٤_ من التنفير استعمال الألفاظ الشنيعة والتشاؤم وسوء الخلق.

٥_ هذه آداب مهمة أمرنا بها رسول الله صلى الله عليه وسلم.

HADEETH 7
The Religion is Easy

Abu Hurayrah (may Allah be pleased with him) reported that the Messenger of Allah (may Allah raise his rank and grant him peace) said:

"The Religion is easy; no one tries to make it difficult, except that it overtakes him."

It was collected by al-Bukhari (39).

POINTS OF BENEFIT FROM THIS HADEETH:

1. *A true believer makes things easy and does not make things hard.*

2. *Whoever does not keep things easy causes harm to himself and others.*

3. *From this ease is that obligations are only based on our abilities. (Review Hadeeth 4.)*

4. *Leaving off religious duties is not the ease which is intended in this hadeeth.*

5. *A believer does not makes things hard on himself with things that he was not asked to do.*

الحديث السابع
الدين يسر

عَنْ أَبِي هُرَيْرَةَ ــرَضِيَ اللهُ عَنْهُ ــ قَالَ: قَالَ رَسُوْلُ اللهِ ــصَلَّى اللهُ عَلَيْهِ وَسَلَّمَ ــ :

«إِنَّ الدِّيْنَ يُسْرٌ، وَلَنْ يُشَادَّ الدِّيْنَ أَحَدٌ إِلَّا غَلَبَهُ.»

أَخْرَجَهُ الْبُخَارِيُّ (٣٩).

ما يستفاد من الحديث:

١_ المؤمن ييسر، ولا يعسر.

٢_ من رفض هذا اليسر تضرر في نفسه، وضر بالآخرين.

٣_ من هذا اليسر: أن الواجب حسب الاستطاعة. [راجع حـ٤]

٤_ ليس ترك الواجبات من اليسر المقصود في هذا الحديث.

٥_ المؤمن لا يكلف نفسه أكثر مما طلب منه.

HADEETH 8
Bid'ah (Innovation)

'A'ishah (may Allah be pleased with her) reported that the Messenger of Allah (may Allah raise his rank and grant him peace) said:

"Whoever does any action which is not in line with our affair will have it rejected."

It was collected by al-Bukhari (2697) and Muslim (1718).

POINTS OF BENEFIT FROM THIS HADEETH:

1. *"Rejected" means: not accepted by Allah.*
2. *Allah does not accept any worship which contradicts the Sunnah.*
3. *Worship must have sincere intentions and it must done according to the Sunnah. (Review Hadeeth 1.)*
4. *Worship which is not according to the Quran and Sunnah is called bid'ah (innovation).*
5. *Every bid'ah is wrong, and there is no good in it.*

الحديث الثامن
الحذر من البدعة

عَنْ عَائِشَةَ ـرَضِيَ اللهُ عَنْهَا ـ قَالَتْ: قَالَ رَسُولُ اللهِ ـصَلَّى اللهُ عَلَيْهِ وَسَلَّمَ ـ :

«مَنْ عَمِلَ عَمَلًا لَيْسَ عَلَيْهِ أَمْرُنَا فَهُوَ رَدٌّ.»

أَخْرَجَهُ الْبُخَارِيُّ (٢٦٩٧) وَمُسْلِمٌ (١٧١٨)، وَاللَّفْظُ لَهُ.

ما يستفاد من الحديث:

١ ـ معنى «رَدٌّ» مردود عند الله، غير مقبول.

٢ ـ لا يقبل الله العبادة المخالفة للسنة.

٣ ـ العبادة الصحيحة لا بد لها من إخلاص النية وموافقة السنة. [راجع حـ١]

٤ ـ العبادة التي لا توافق القرآن والسنة تسمى بدعة.

٥ ـ كل بدعة خطأ ولا خير فيها.

PART TWO

THE BEST

DEEDS

البَابُ الثَّانِي

أَفْضَلُ الأَعْمَالِ

HADEETH 9
The Best People

'Uthman (may Allah be pleased with him) reported that the Messenger of Allah (may Allah raise his rank and grant him peace) said:

"The best of you are those who learn the Quran and teach it."

It was collected by al-Bukhari (5027).

POINTS OF BENEFIT FROM THIS HADEETH:

1. *The Quran is the Book of Allah and His Speech. It is not created, and it is not like people's speech.*

2. *One of the best deeds is to learn the Quran with a good intention.*

3. *One of the best deeds is to teach the Quran with a good intention.*

4. *We love and respect the Quran teachers and their students.*

5. *The Quran has a very important place in the lives of the believers.*

الحديث التاسع
خير الناس

عَنْ عُثْمَانَ ـرَضِيَ اللهُ عَنْهُ ـ قَالَ: قَالَ رَسُولُ اللهِ ـصَلَّى اللهُ عَلَيْهِ وَسَلَّمَ ـ:

«خَيْرُكُمْ مَنْ تَعَلَّمَ الْقُرْآنَ وَعَلَّمَهُ.»

أَخْرَجَهُ الْبُخَارِيُّ (٥٠٢٧).

ما يستفاد من الحديث:

١ _ القرآن كتاب الله وكلامه، غير مخلوق، وليس هو مثل كلام الناس.

٢ _ من أفضل الأعمال أن نتعلم كتاب الله بنية حسنة.

٣ _ من أفضل الأعمال تعليم الناس القرآن بنية حسنة.

٤ _ نحب ونحترم المعلمين للقرآن وتلاميذهم.

٥ _ القرآن له دور عظيم في حياة المؤمنين.

HADEETH 10
You and the Quran

Abu Malik al-Ash'ari (may Allah be pleased with him) reported that the Messenger of Allah (may Allah raise his rank and grant him peace) said:

"The Quran is a proof for you or against you."

It was collected by Muslim (223).

POINTS OF BENEFIT FROM THIS HADEETH:

1. *The Book of Allah can be a source of reward for us or a source of punishment.*

2. *Whoever leaves the Quran and does not learn it, the Quran is a proof against him.*

3. *Whoever learns the Quran but does not act by it, the Quran is proof against him.*

4. *Whoever learns the Quran and acts by it, but with bad intentions, the Quran is a proof against him.*

5. *Whoever learns the Quran and acts by it sincerely and in line with the Sunnah, the Quran is a proof for him.*

الحديث العاشر
أنت والقرآن

عَنْ أَبِي مَالِكٍ الْأَشْعَرِيِّ ــرَضِيَ اللهُ عَنْهُ ــ قَالَ: قَالَ رَسُولُ اللهِ ــصَلَّى اللهُ عَلَيْهِ وَسَلَّمَ ــ :

«الْقُرْآنُ حُجَّةٌ لَكَ أَوْ عَلَيْكَ.»

أَخْرَجَهُ مُسْلِمٌ (٢٢٣).

ما يستفاد من الحديث:

١ _ قد يكون كتاب الله سبب ثواب لنا أو سبب عذابنا.

٢ _ من ترك القرآن ولم يتعلمه فالقرآن حجة عليه يوم القيامة.

٣ _ من تعلم القرآن ولم يعمل به فالقرآن حجة عليه.

٤ _ من تعلم القرآن وعمل به بنية فاسدة فالقرآن حجة عليه.

٥ _ من تعلم القرآن وعمل به بإخلاص وموافقة السنة فالقرآن حجة له.

HADEETH 11
Fiqh in the Religion

Mu'awiyah ibn Abee Sufyan (may Allah be pleased with him) reported that the Messenger of Allah (may Allah raise his rank and grant him peace) said:

"When Allah wants good for someone, He gives him *Fiqh* in the Religion."

It was collected by al-Bukhari (71) and Muslim (1037).

POINTS OF BENEFIT FROM THIS HADEETH:

1. *Fiqh in the Religion is the correct understanding of the Quran and Sunnah and acting by it.*

2. *Fiqh is a gift from Allah; He gives it to those He wants good for.*

3. *A true believer asks Allah for Fiqh in the Religion.*

4. *Allah sent the Quran to be understood and acted upon.*

5. *A true believer loves the scholars and respects them, because Allah loves them and wants good for them.*

الحديث الحادي عشر
الفقه في الدين

عَنْ مُعَاوِيَةَ بْنِ أَبِي سُفْيَانَ ـرَضِيَ اللهُ عَنْهُ ـ قَالَ: قَالَ رَسُولُ اللهِ ـصَلَّى اللهُ عَلَيْهِ وَسَلَّمَ ـ:

«مَنْ يُرِدِ اللهُ بِهِ خَيْرًا يُفَقِّهْهُ فِي الدِّينِ.»

أَخْرَجَهُ الْبُخَارِيُّ (٧١) وَمُسْلِمٌ (١٠٣٧).

ما يستفاد من الحديث:

١ـ الفقه في الدين هو الفهم الصحيح للقرآن مع العمل به.

٢ـ الفقه منة من الله يعطيها من أراد له خيرا.

٣ـ المؤمن يسأل الله الفقه في الدين.

٤ـ أنزل الله القرآن ليفهمه الناس ويطبقوه.

٥ـ المؤمن يحب الفقهاء ويحترمهم، لأن الله يحبهم ويريد لهم خيرا.

HADEETH 12
The People Allah Loves

Sa'd ibn Abee Waqqas (may Allah be pleased with him) reported that the Messenger of Allah (may Allah raise his rank and grant him peace) said:

"Allah loves the pious, content, humble worshipper."

It was collected by Muslim (2965).

POINTS OF BENEFIT FROM THIS HADEETH:

1. *Allah loves the believers who understand the Religion and act by it.*

2. *The Messenger (may Allah raise his rank and grant him peace) taught us about the actions and manners which Allah loves.*

3. *A pious person has taqwa, which is to fear Allah and to do your religious duties and avoid haram.*

4. *Being rich is not by money; a truly rich person is content with what Allah has given him.*

5. *A humble person is sincere and does not want to be known or famous.*

الحديث الثاني عشر
صفات من يحبه الله

عَنْ سَعْدِ بْنِ أَبِي وَقَّاصٍ ـرَضِيَ اللهُ عَنْهُ ـ قَالَ: قَالَ رَسُولُ اللهِ ـ صَلَّى اللهُ عَلَيْهِ وَسَلَّمَ ـ:

«إِنَّ اللهَ يُحِبُّ الْعَبْدَ التَّقِيَّ الْغَنِيَّ الْخَفِيَّ.»

أَخْرَجَهُ مُسْلِمٌ (٢٩٦٥).

ما يستفاد من الحديث:

١ _ يحب الله المؤمنين الذين يفهمون الدين ويعملون به.

٢ _ يعلمنا الرسول صلى الله عليه وسلم ما يحبه الله من الأعمال والأخلاق.

٣ _ التقي صاحب التقوى، وهو الخوف من الله وأداء الواجب وترك الحرام.

٤ _ الغني ليس بالمال، بل الغني هو الذي يرضى بما آتاه الله.

٥ _ الخفي هو صاحب الإخلاص الذي لا يحب الظهور والشهرة.

HADEETH 13
Praying for Good Manners

Ibn Mas'ud (may Allah be pleased with him) reported that the Messenger of Allah (may Allah raise his rank and grant him peace) used to say:

"O Allah! I do ask You for guidance, piety, chastity, and contentment."

It was collected by Muslim (2721).

POINTS OF BENEFIT FROM THIS HADEETH:

1. *A true believer calls upon Allah and asks for things that Allah loves.*
2. *A true believer asks Allah for guidance to the truth and firmness upon it.*
3. *Piety is to fear Allah, obey Him, and be aware of Him in all our words and deeds.*
4. *Chastity is being shy in words and deeds, and being far away from nasty behavior.*
5. *Contentment is to be happy with what Allah has given us and to rely upon Him alone.*

الحديث الثالث عشر
إصلاح الأخلاق بالدعاء

عَنِ ابْنِ مَسْعُودٍ ـرَضِيَ اللهُ عَنْهُ ـ: عَنِ النَّبِيِّ ـصَلَّى اللهُ عَلَيْهِ وَسَلَّمَ ـ، أَنَّهُ كَانَ يَقُولُ:

«اللَّهُمَّ إِنِّي أَسْأَلُكَ الْهُدَى وَالتُّقَى وَالْعَفَافَ وَالْغِنَى.»

أَخْرَجَهُ مُسْلِمٌ (٢٧٢١).

ما يستفاد من الحديث:

١ _ المؤمن يدعو الله ويطلب الصفات التي يحبها الله.

٢ _ المؤمن يسأل الله الهداية للحق والثبات عليه.

٣ _ التقى هو التقوى وهو الخوف من الله وطاعته ومراقبته في القول والعمل.

٤ _ العفاف هو الحياء في القول والعمل والبعد عن الفواحش.

٥ _ الغنى الرضا عن ما رزقنا الله واعتمادنا عليه والاستغناء به عن غيره.

HADEETH 14
Being Content

Abu Hurayrah (may Allah be pleased with him) reported that the Messenger of Allah (may Allah raise his rank and grant him peace) said:

"Real contentment is the contentment of the soul."

It was collected by al-Bukhari (6446) and Muslim (1051).

POINTS OF BENEFIT FROM THIS HADEETH:

1. *Allah loves content people, so we ask Allah for souls which are content.*

2. *Being content with Allah does not mean having lots of money like many people think.*

3. *Some people have lots of money, houses, and cars, but their souls are poor.*

4. *Some people do not have a lot of worldly things, but their souls are rich.*

5. *This world is limited and it comes to an end; only our deeds remain on the Day of Judgment.*

الحديث الرابع عشر
الغنى

عَنْ أَبِي هُرَيْرَةَ ـرَضِيَ اللهُ عَنْهُ ـ قَالَ: قَالَ رَسُولُ اللهِ ـصَلَّى اللهُ عَلَيْهِ وَسَلَّمَ ـ :

«الْغِنَى غِنَى النَّفْسِ.»

أَخْرَجَهُ الْبُخَارِيُّ (٦٤٤٦) وَمُسْلِمٌ (١٠٥١).

ما يستفاد من الحديث:

١_ يحب الله العبد الغني، فنسأل الله غنى أنفسنا.

٢_ ليس الغنى عند الله كثرة المال كما يزعمه أكثر الناس.

٣_ هناك من جمع الأموال الكثيرة والبيوت والسيارات وهو فقير في نفسه.

٤_ هناك مقلون لا يملكون الكثير من الدنيا، لكنهم أغنياء في نفوسهم.

٥_ الدنيا فانية فتنتهي، ولا يبقى إلا الأعمال والأقوال يوم القيامة.

HADEETH 15
Focus on the Hereafter

Ibn 'Umar (may Allah be pleased with him) reported that the Messenger of Allah (may Allah raise his rank and grant him peace) grabbed his shoulder and said:

"Be in this world like a stranger or a traveler."

It was collected by al-Bukhari (6416).

POINTS OF BENEFIT FROM THIS HADEETH:

1. *If our souls are content, our hearts will be focused on the Hereafter more than this world.*

2. *When a person is focused on the Hereafter, he does not care if the people approve of him, so he is a stranger among them.*

3. *A traveler stops at a place to get some rest, and then he moves on.*

4. *A traveler only takes things which will help him and not slow him down on his trip.*

5. *Many people might laugh at strangers, but that does not hurt them.*

الحديث الخامس عشر
الزهد

عَنِ ابْنِ عُمَرَ ـ رَضِيَ اللهُ عَنْهُمَا ـ قَالَ: أَخَذَ رَسُولُ اللهِ ـ صَلَّى اللهُ عَلَيْهِ وَسَلَّمَ ـ بِمَنْكِبِي، فَقَالَ:

«كُنْ فِي الدُّنْيَا كَأَنَّكَ غَرِيبٌ أَوْ عَابِرُ سَبِيلٍ.»

أَخْرَجَهُ الْبُخَارِيُّ (٦٤١٦).

ما يستفاد من الحديث:

١ _ الغني في نفسه يتعلق قلبه بأمور الآخرة أكثر من أمور الدنيا.

٢ _ الذي نيته الآخرة يغنيه الله عن رضى الناس فيكون فيهم غريبا.

٣ _ عابر السبيل هو المسافر الذي يقف في مكان ويستريح قليلا ثم يرتحل.

٤ _ المسافر يأخذ من الدنيا ما ينفعه ولا يؤخره عن مواصلة السير.

٥ _ الغرباء قد يستهزئ بهم كثير من الناس، ولا يضرهم ذلك.

HADEETH 16
Islam is Strange

Abu Hurayrah (may Allah be pleased with him) reported that the Messenger of Allah (may Allah raise his rank and grant him peace) said:

"Islam started as something strange, and it will return to being strange, so *Toobaa* to the strangers."

It was collected by Muslim (145). ***"Toobaa"*** means: good news.

POINTS OF BENEFIT FROM THIS HADEETH:

1. *The Prophet (may Allah raise his rank and grant him peace) and his companions were a small group of people in the first years of Islam.*

2. *When most people are evil in any time or place, the good people are strangers.*

3. *A true believer is not tricked by large numbers of evil people or small numbers of good people.*

4. *When you see a stranger (a good Muslim among bad people), then give him good news and do not treat him badly.*

5. *True believers are a small number of people in this world where most people do not believe in Allah or obey Him.*

الحديث السادس عشر
غربة الإسلام

عَنْ أَبِي هُرَيْرَةَ ـرَضِيَ اللهُ عَنْهُ ـ قَالَ: قَالَ رَسُولُ اللهِ ـصَلَّى اللهُ عَلَيْهِ وَسَلَّمَـ :

«بَدَأَ الْإِسْلَامُ غَرِيبًا، وَسَيَعُودُ كَمَا بَدَأَ غَرِيبًا، فَطُوبَى لِلْغُرَبَاءِ.»

أَخْرَجَهُ مُسْلِمٌ (١٤٥). وَمَعْنَى «طُوبَى»: بُشْرَى.

ما يستفاد من الحديث:

١_ كان النبي صلى الله عليه وسلم وأصحابه قلة في قومهم في أول الإسلام.

٢_ إذا فسد أكثر الناس في أي مكان أو زمان فالصالحون هم الغرباء.

٣_ لا يغتر المؤمن بكثرة الهالكين، ولا بقلة الناجين.

٤_ إذا رأيت غريبا بغربة الإسلام فبشره ولا تنفره. [راجع ح٦]

٥_ المؤمنون قلة في هذه الدنيا، فأكثر الناس لا يؤمنون بالله ولا يطيعونه.

HADEETH 17
Being Upright

Sufyan ibn 'Abdillah ath-Thaqafi (may Allah be pleased with him) said to the Prophet (may Allah raise his rank and grant him peace): O Messenger of Allah! Tell me something about Islam that I will not need to ask anyone after you? He replied:

"Say: 'I believe in Allah,' and then be upright."

It was collected by Muslim (38).

POINTS OF BENEFIT FROM THIS HADEETH:

1. *Being upright when the people are evil is from the strangeness of Islam.*

2. *A true believer works hard to protect his tongue from saying things which are not appropriate.*

3. *Islam is about words and deeds, open and secret. (Review Hadeeth 2.)*

4. *Those who practice this hadeeth, **"Angels come down to them and say 'Do not fear or be sad; good news of Paradise..."** (Quran 41:30)*

5. *Part of being upright is to do good deeds **regularly**.*

الحديث السابع عشر
الاستقامة

عَنْ سُفْيَانَ بْنِ عَبْدِ اللهِ الثَّقَفِيِّ ـرَضِيَ اللهُ عَنْهُ ـ قَالَ: قُلْتُ: يَا رَسُولَ اللهِ! قُلْ لِي فِي الْإِسْلَامِ قَوْلًا لَا أَسْأَلُ عَنْهُ أَحَدًا بَعْدَكَ؟ قَالَ:

«قُلْ: آمَنْتُ بِاللهِ، فَاسْتَقِمْ.»

أَخْرَجَهُ مُسْلِمٌ (٣٨).

ما يستفاد من الحديث:

١_ الاستقامة عند فساد الناس من الغربة الممدوحة.

٢_ المؤمن يجتهد في إصلاح لسانه وصيانته عما لا يليق به.

٣_ الإسلام أقوال وأعمال ظاهرة وباطنة. (راجع حـ٢)

٤_ الذين يطبقون هذا الحديث {تتنزل عليهم الملائكة ألا تخافوا ولا تحزنوا وأبشروا بالجنة...} [فصلت:٣٠]

٥_ من الاستقامة أن يداوم المؤمن على الأعمال الصالحة.

HADEETH 18
Being Consistent

'A'ishah (may Allah be pleased with her) reported that the Messenger of Allah (may Allah raise his rank and grant him peace) said:

"The most beloved deeds to Allah, the Most High, are those done consistently, even if they are not many."

It was collected by al-Bukhari (6464) and Muslim (783).

POINTS OF BENEFIT FROM THIS HADEETH:

1. *Allah loves when a worshipper is consistent in good things and in being upright.*

2. *A good deed might be small, but Allah loves it because of how the believer is consistent with it.*

3. *Islam is a religion of deeds; it is not just beliefs and statements.*

4. *Allah really loves some people and their deeds with a real kind of love that suits Him.*

5. *Deeds are on different levels with Allah – Some are bad; some are even worse. Some are good; some are even better.*

الحديث الثامن عشر
المداومة على الخير

عَنْ عَائِشَةَ ـرَضِيَ اللهُ عَنْهَاـ قَالَتْ: قَالَ رَسُولُ اللهِ ـصَلَّى اللهُ عَلَيْهِ وَسَلَّمَـ:

«أَحَبُّ الْأَعْمَالِ إِلَى اللهِ تَعَالَى أَدْوَمُهَا وَإِنْ قَلَّ.»

أَخْرَجَهُ الْبُخَارِيُّ (٦٤٦٤) وَمُسْلِمٌ (٧٨٣)، وَاللَّفْظُ لَهُ.

ما يستفاد من الحديث:

١_ يحب الله استمرار عبده على الخير والاستقامة.

٢_ قد يكون العمل قليلا، لكن الله يحبه لاستمرار المؤمن عليه.

٣_ دين الإسلام دين عمل، وليس بمجرد عقائد وأقوال.

٤_ الله يحب بعض الناس وأعمالهم محبة حقيقية تليق به.

٥_ الأعمال متفاوتة عند الله: منها سيء وأسوأ، ومنها فاضل وأفضل.

HADEETH 19
Prayer & Kindness to Parents

Ibn Mas'ud (may Allah be pleased with him) reported that the Messenger of Allah (may Allah raise his rank and grant him peace) said:

"The best deeds are prayer in its time and kindness to parents."

It was collected by al-Bukhari (7534) and Muslim (85).

POINTS OF BENEFIT FROM THIS HADEETH:

1. *Being consistent is especially important when it comes to prayer and kindness to parents.*

2. *Prayers have certain times set by Allah.*

3. *Allah loves that we offer our prayers in the first part of their times.*

4. *Kindness to parents includes obeying them, serving them, and having good manners with them.*

5. *The worst deeds are not praying or delaying the prayers outside of their times, and bad behavior with parents.*

الحديث التاسع عشر
الصلاة وبر الوالدين

عَنِ ابْنِ مَسْعُودٍ _رَضِيَ اللهُ عَنْهُ_ قَالَ: قَالَ رَسُوْلُ اللهِ _صَلَّى اللهُ عَلَيْهِ وَسَلَّمَ_:

«أَفْضَلُ الأَعْمَالِ الصَّلَاةُ لِوَقْتِهَا، وَبِرُّ الْوَالِدَيْنِ.»

أَخْرَجَهُ الْبُخَارِيُّ (٧٥٣٤) وَمُسْلِمٌ (٨٥)، وَاللَّفْظُ لَهُ.

ما يستفاد من الحديث:

١_ تتأكد المداومة على أداء الصلوات والإحسان في معاملة الوالدين.

٢_ الصلوات لها أوقات خاصة شرعها الله.

٣_ يحب الله أن نبادر إلى أداء الصلوات في أول أوقاتها.

٤_ بر الوالدين يكون بطاعتهما وخدمتهما والتأدب معهما.

٥_ من شر الأعمال: ترك الصلوات أو تأخيرها عن أوقاتها، والإساءة إلى الوالدين.

PART THREE

HONESTY

الْبَابُ الثَّالِثُ

الصِّدْقُ

HADEETH 20
The Major Sins

Abu Bakrah (may Allah be pleased with him) reported that the Messenger of Allah (may Allah raise his rank and grant him peace) said:

"The worst major sins are setting up partners with Allah, bad treatment of parents, and false speech."

It was collected by al-Bukhari (6919) and Muslim (87).

POINTS OF BENEFIT FROM THIS HADEETH:

1. *The worst sins are the major sins; a true believer works hard to stay away from them.*

2. *The worship of Allah alone is the most important duty and the reason why people were created.*

3. *Shirk is to direct any kind of worship to someone other than Allah.*

4. *Bad treatment of parents is one of the worst sins.*

5. *False speech is lies; a believer hates it and does not want to see it or support it.*

الحديث العشرون
الكبائر

عَنْ أَبِي بَكْرَةَ ـرَضِيَ اللهُ عَنْهُ ـ قَالَ: قَالَ رَسُولُ اللهِ ـصَلَّى اللهُ عَلَيْهِ وَسَلَّمَ ـ :

«أَكْبَرُ الْكَبَائِرِ: الْإِشْرَاكُ بِاللهِ، وَعُقُوقُ الْوَالِدَيْنِ، وَشَهَادَةُ الزُّورِ.»

أَخْرَجَهُ الْبُخَارِيُّ (٦٩١٩) وَمُسْلِمٌ (٨٧)، وَهَذَا لَفْظُ الْبُخَارِيِّ.

ما يستفاد من الحديث:

١_ شر السيئات هي كبائر الذنوب، فالمؤمن يجتهد في اجتنابها.

٢_ عبادة الله وحده أول الواجبات وسبب خلق الناس جميعا.

٣_ الإشراك أو الشرك هو صرف شيء من العبادة لغير الله.

٤_ عقوق الوالدين هو الإساءة إليهما، وهو من أكبر الذنوب الكبيرة.

٥_ الزور هو الباطل والكذب، فالمؤمن ينكره ولا يشهده، أو يشهد عليه.

HADEETH 21
Hypocrisy

Abu Hurayrah (may Allah be pleased with him) reported that the Messenger of Allah (may Allah raise his rank and grant him peace) said:

"The signs of a hypocrite are three: when he speaks, he lies; when he promises something, he breaks his promise; and when he is trusted, he betrays."

It was collected by al-Bukhari (33) and Muslim (59).

POINTS OF BENEFIT FROM THIS HADEETH:

1. *A hypocrite is someone who openly seems good, but he hides evil inside.*

2. *A true believer stays away from major sins, like the worst of them: the actions of the hypocrites.*

3. *Lying is haram and one of the major sins; it is from the actions of the hypocrites.*

4. *Breaking promises is haram and one of the major sins; it is from the actions of the hypocrites.*

5. *Betrayal is haram and one of the major sins; it is from the actions of the hypocrites.*

الحديث الحادي والعشرون
النفاق

عَنْ أَبِي هُرَيْرَةَ ـرَضِيَ اللهُ عَنْهُ ـ قَالَ: قَالَ رَسُولُ اللهِ ـصَلَّى اللهُ عَلَيْهِ وَسَلَّمَ ـ :

«آيَةُ الْمُنَافِقِ ثَلاَثٌ: إِذَا حَدَّثَ كَذَبَ، وَإِذَا وَعَدَ أَخْلَفَ، وَإِذَا اؤْتُمِنَ خَانَ.»

أَخْرَجَهُ الْبُخَارِيُّ (٣٣) وَمُسْلِمٌ (٥٩).

ما يستفاد من الحديث:

١_ المنافق هو الذي يظهر الخير ويخفي الشر.

٢_ المؤمن يبتعد عن الكبائر، ومن أشنعها: صفات المنافقين.

٣_ الكذب حرام من الكبائر، وهو من صفات المنافقين.

٤_ إخلاف الوعد حرام من الكبائر، وهو من صفات المنافقين.

٥_ خيانة الأمانة حرام من الكبائر، وهي من صفات المنافقين.

HADEETH 22
Lying on the Prophet

Abu Hurayrah (may Allah be pleased with him) reported that the Messenger of Allah (may Allah raise his rank and grant him peace) said:

"Whoever lies on me intentionally will take his seat in the Hellfire."

It was collected by al-Bukhari (110) and Muslim (3).

POINTS OF BENEFIT FROM THIS HADEETH:

1. *Lying is a haram major sin; lying on the Messenger of Allah (may Allah raise his rank and grant him peace) is even more dangerous.*

2. *Lying on the Messenger of Allah (may Allah raise his rank and grant him peace) could lead to changes in the Religion of Allah.*

3. *Whoever lies on the Messenger of Allah (may Allah raise his rank and grant him peace) goes to Hell.*

4. *A true believer is afraid to make a mistake when quoting the Sunnah, so the Quran is even more serious.*

5. *This fear does not stop a believer from spreading the Sunnah.*

الحديث الثاني والعشرون
الكذب على النبي

عَنْ أَبِي هُرَيْرَةَ ـ رَضِيَ اللهُ عَنْهُ ـ قَالَ: قَالَ رَسُولُ اللهِ ـ صَلَّى اللهُ عَلَيْهِ وَسَلَّمَ ـ :

«مَنْ كَذَبَ عَلَيَّ مُتَعَمِّدًا فَلْيَتَبَوَّأْ مَقْعَدَهُ مِنَ النَّارِ.»

أَخْرَجَهُ الْبُخَارِيُّ (١١٠) وَمُسْلِمٌ (٣).

ما يستفاد من الحديث:

١ _ الكذب حرام من الكبائر، والكذب على رسول الله صلى الله عليه وسلم أشد.

٢ _ الكذب على رسول الله صلى الله عليه وسلم يؤدي إلى التغيير في دين الله.

٣ _ من كذب على رسول الله صلى الله عليه وسلم يدخل النار.

٤ _ المؤمن الصادق يخاف أن يخطئ فيما يرويه من السنة، فالقرآن من باب أولى.

٥ _ هذا الخوف لا يمنع المؤمن من نشر السنة.

PART FOUR

CALLING
TO THE WAY
OF ALLAH

الْبَابُ الرَّابِعُ

الدَّعْوَةُ

إِلَى اللَّهِ

HADEETH 23
Sharing Islam

'Abdullah ibn 'Amr (may Allah be pleased with him) reported that the Messenger of Allah (may Allah raise his rank and grant him peace) said:

"Share from me [what I teach, to others], even if it is just one verse."

It was collected by al-Bukhari (3461).

POINTS OF BENEFIT FROM THIS HADEETH:

1. *It is not allowed to hide what we know from the Quran and Sunnah.*

2. *Sharing Islam with others is a duty on us.*

3. *A true believer shares what he knows about Allah's Religion, even if it is something small.*

4. *Calling to Allah's Way includes teaching people what they do not know and reminding them about what they already know.*

5. *A true believer is sincere and hopes for reward from Allah when sharing His Religion with others.*

الحديث الثالث والعشرون
نشر الدين

عَنْ عَبْدِ اللهِ بْنِ عَمْرٍو ــ رَضِيَ اللهُ عَنْهُمَا ــ قَالَ: قَالَ رَسُولُ اللهِ ــ صَلَّى اللهُ عَلَيْهِ وَسَلَّمَ ــ :

«بَلِّغُواْ عَنِّي، وَلَوْ آيَةً.»

أَخْرَجَهُ الْبُخَارِيُّ (٣٤٦١).

ما يستفاد من الحديث:

١ ــ لا يجوز كتمان علم القرآن والسنة.

٢ ــ تبليغ الدين الإسلامي واجب.

٣ ــ المؤمن يبلغ من دين الله ما يعلمه، ولو كان شيئا يسيرا.

٤ ــ الدعوة إلى الله تعليم الناس ما يجهلون وتذكيرهم بما يعلمون.

٥ ــ المؤمن يخلص نيته ويرجو ثواب الله في تبليغ دينه.

HADEETH 24
Rewards for Guiding People

Sahl ibn Sa'd (may Allah be pleased with him) reported that the Messenger of Allah (may Allah raise his rank and grant him peace) said:

"For Allah to guide just one person by way of you is better for you than having red camels."

It was collected by al-Bukhari (3701) and Muslim (2406). **"Red camels"** means the best kinds of wealth.

POINTS OF BENEFIT FROM THIS HADEETH:

1. *The rewards of Allah are great, even for guiding a single person.*

2. *Guiding the hearts is only for Allah.*

3. ***"You prefer this worldly life, while the Hereafter is better and more lasting."*** *[87:16-17]*

4. *Allah is generous; He gives great rewards for someone who does basic things, if they are sincere.*

5. *Calling to the way of Allah is by speech and action.*

الحديث الرابع والعشرون
ثواب الدعوة

عَنْ سَهْلِ بْنِ سَعْدٍ ــرَضِيَ اللهُ عَنْهُمَا ــ قَالَ: قَالَ رَسُولُ اللهِ ــصَلَّى اللهُ عَلَيْهِ وَسَلَّمَ ــ :

«لَأَنْ يَهْدِيَ اللهُ بِكَ رَجُلًا وَاحِدًا خَيْرٌ لَكَ مِنْ أَنْ يَكُونَ لَكَ حُمْرُ النَّعَمِ.»

أَخْرَجَهُ الْبُخَارِيُّ (٣٧٠١) وَمُسْلِمٌ (٢٤٠٦). وَ«حُمْرُ النَّعَمِ»: أَفْضَلُ الْأَمْوَالِ.

ما يستفاد من الحديث:

١ ـ ثواب الله عظيم، حتى في إرشاد الشخص الواحد.

٢ ـ هداية القلوب بيد الله وحده.

٣ ـ {بل تؤثرون الحياة الدنيا والآخرة خير وأبقى}

٤ ـ الله كريم حيث جعل ثوابا كبيرا جدا لمن قام بعمل يسير بإخلاص له.

٥ ـ الدعوة إلى الله تكون بالقول والعمل.

HADEETH 25
Rewards for Guiding People

Abu Mas'ud al-Ansari (may Allah be pleased with him) reported that the Messenger of Allah (may Allah raise his rank and grant him peace) said:

"Whoever guides [others] to something good shall have a reward like the one who does it."

It was collected by Muslim (1893).

POINTS OF BENEFIT FROM THIS HADEETH:

1. *Islam is about actions; he said,* **"A reward like the one who <u>does</u> it,"** *and he did not say, "Like the one who <u>listened</u>."*

2. *Leading people into good things has a great reward which grows.*

3. *Allah is Generous, as He gives ongoing rewards for a single action.*

4. *A true believer corrects himself first; whenever his advice to others matches his own practice, it works better.*

5. *A true believer learns and practices, for his own benefit, and for the benefit of others, too.*

الحديث الخامس والعشرون
ثواب الدعوة

عَنْ أَبِي مَسْعُودٍ الْأَنْصَارِيِّ ـ رَضِيَ اللهُ عَنْهُ ـ ، قَالَ: قَالَ رَسُولُ اللهِ ـ صَلَّى اللهُ عَلَيْهِ وَسَلَّمَ ـ :

«مَنْ دَلَّ عَلَى خَيْرٍ فَلَهُ مِثْلُ أَجْرِ فَاعِلِهِ.»

أَخْرَجَهُ مُسْلِمٌ (١٨٩٣).

ما يستفاد من الحديث:

١ _ الإسلام دين عمل وتطبيق، فإنه قال "أجر فاعله"، وما قال: "سامعه".

٢ _ الدلالة على الخير أجرها عظيم مضاعف.

٣ _ الله كريم حيث جعل أجرا مستمرا على العمل الواحد.

٤ _ المؤمن يصلح نفسه أولا، فإن كان إرشاده لغيره موافقا لقدوته، فناجح.

٥ _ المؤمن يتعلم ويعمل ويريد لغيره ما يريده لنفسه من الخير.

PART FIVE

ISLAMIC

BROTHERHOOD

البَابُ الخَامِسُ

الأُخُوَّةُ

الإِسلَامِيَّةُ

HADEETH 26
Wanting Good for Others

Anas (may Allah be pleased with him) reported that the Messenger of Allah (may Allah raise his rank and grant him peace) said:

"None of you truly believes until he loves for his brother what he loves for himself."

It was collected by al-Bukhari (13) and Muslim (45).

POINTS OF BENEFIT FROM THIS HADEETH:

1. *A true believer is a brother to another believer; he leads him into what is good.*

2. *A true believer is not selfish; he cares about others.*

3. *We should deal with people how we would like them to deal with us.*

4. *Love is part of faith.*

5. *Believers are brothers; they help one another.*

الحديث السادس والعشرون
إرادة الخير للغير

عَنْ أَنَسٍ ـرَضِيَ اللهُ عَنْهُ ـ قَالَ: قَالَ رَسُولُ اللهِ ـصَلَّى اللهُ عَلَيْهِ وَسَلَّمَ ـ :

«لَا يُؤْمِنُ أَحَدُكُمْ حَتَّى يُحِبَّ لِأَخِيهِ مَا يُحِبُّ لِنَفْسِهِ.»

أَخْرَجَهُ الْبُخَارِيُّ (١٣) وَمُسْلِمٌ (٤٥).

ما يستفاد من الحديث:

١ ـ المؤمن أخ المؤمن، يدل أخيه على الخير.

٢ ـ لا يكون المؤمن بخيلا أنانيا.

٣ ـ نتعامل مع الآخرين بأسلوب حسن كما نحب أن يتعاملوا معنا.

٤ ـ المحبة من الإيمان.

٥ ـ المؤمنون إخوة يساعد بعضهم بعضا.

HADEETH 27
Believers are Brothers

Abu Moosa (may Allah be pleased with him) reported that the Messenger of Allah (may Allah raise his rank and grant him peace) said:

"A believer with another believer is like how some parts of a building strengthen other parts."

It was collected by al-Bukhari (2446) and Muslim (2585).

POINTS OF BENEFIT FROM THIS HADEETH:

1. *Believers are brothers; they strengthen one another.*

2. *Islam is a community-based religion.*

3. *Believers strengthen one another in good things, not in evil things.*

4. *Believers are many people found all over the world, yet they are still like one single structure together.*

5. *Believers cooperate with one another in all things which Allah loves.*

الحديث السابع والعشرون
المؤمنون إخوة

عَنْ أَبِي مُوسَى ـرَضِيَ اللهُ عَنْهُـ قَالَ: قَالَ رَسُولُ اللهِ ـصَلَّى اللهُ عَلَيْهِ وَسَلَّمَـ :

«الْمُؤْمِنُ لِلْمُؤْمِنِ كَالْبُنْيَانِ، يَشُدُّ بَعْضُهُ بَعْضًا.»

أَخْرَجَهُ الْبُخَارِيُّ (٢٤٤٦) وَمُسْلِمٌ (٢٥٨٥).

ما يستفاد من الحديث:

١_ المؤمنون إخوة يقوي بعضهم بعضا.

٢_ الإسلام دين اجتماعي.

٣_ يشد بعض المؤمنين بعضا في الخير لا في الشر.

٤_ المؤمنون عددهم كثير وهم منتشرون في البلاد، لكنهم كبنيان واحد.

٥_ المؤمنون يساعد بعضهم بعضا فيما يحبه الله.

HADEETH 28
Helping Someone in Need

Abu Hurayrah (may Allah be pleased with him) reported that the Messenger of Allah (may Allah raise his rank and grant him peace) said:

"Allah aids a person, so long as that person aids his brother."

It was collected by Muslim (2699).

POINTS OF BENEFIT FROM THIS HADEETH:

1. *Allah helps a believer, so long as he helps his brothers and sisters.*

2. *He did not say that Allah sends an angel to help him; Allah Himself will aid him!*

3. *We are always in need of our Lord's help.*

4. *If Allah helps a person, no one could harm him.*

5. *Helping people sometimes means correcting mistakes and advising them.*

الحديث الثامن والعشرون
إعانة المحتاج

عَنْ أَبِي هُرَيْرَةَ _رَضِيَ اللهُ عَنْهُ_ قَالَ: قَالَ رَسُولُ اللهِ _صَلَّى اللهُ عَلَيْهِ وَسَلَّمَ_ :

«اللهُ فِي عَوْنِ الْعَبْدِ مَا كَانَ الْعَبْدُ فِي عَوْنِ أَخِيهِ.»

أَخْرَجَهُ مُسْلِمٌ (٢٦٩٩).

ما يستفاد من الحديث:

١ _ الله يعين المؤمن بشرط أنه يساعد إخوانه وأخواته.

٢ _ ما قال إنه يرسل ملكا ليعينه، بل الله نفسه في عونه!

٣ _ نحن في حاجة إلى ربنا دائما.

٤ _ من كان الله في عونه، فلا أحد يستطيع أن يضره.

٥ _ إعانة الناس أحيانا تصحيح الخطأ والنصيحة.

HADEETH 29
Different Ways of Helping

Anas (may Allah be pleased with him) reported that the Messenger of Allah (may Allah raise his rank and grant him peace) said:

"Help your brother, whether he is an oppressor or a victim."

It was collected by al-Bukhari (2443).

POINTS OF BENEFIT FROM THIS HADEETH:

1. *Believers are brothers who help one another.*

2. *Believers are fair, and they avoid oppression.*

3. *A true believer helps his brother when he is a victim by defending him.*

4. *A true believer helps his brother when he is an oppressor by advising him and forbidding him from evil.*

5. ***"Allah loves those who are fair"*** *[49:9], and **"Allah does not love oppressors."** [3:57]*

الحديث التاسع والعشرون
أنواع النصر

عَنْ أَنَسٍ ـرَضِيَ اللهُ عَنْهُ ـ قَالَ: قَالَ رَسُولُ اللهِ ـصَلَّى اللهُ عَلَيْهِ وَسَلَّمَ ـ :

«انْصُرْ أَخَاكَ ظَالِمًا أَوْ مَظْلُوْمًا.»

أَخْرَجَهُ الْبُخَارِيُّ (٢٤٤٣).

ما يستفاد من الحديث:

١_ المؤمنون إخوة ينصر بعضهم بعضا.

٢_ المؤمنون عدول لا يظلمون الناس.

٣_ ينصر المؤمن أخاه المظلوم بالدفاع عنه.

٤_ ينصر المؤمن أخاه الظالم بالنصيحة ونهيه عن ظلمه.

٥_ {إن الله يحب المقسطين}؛ {والله لا يحب الظالمين}

HADEETH 30
Oppression

Ibn 'Umar (may Allah be pleased with him) reported that the Messenger of Allah (may Allah raise his rank and grant him peace) said:

"Oppression is many layers of darkness on the Day of Judgment."

It was collected by al-Bukhari (2447) and Muslim (2579).

POINTS OF BENEFIT FROM THIS HADEETH:

1. *How can you help your oppressive brother? Remind him about this hadeeth!*

2. *Oppression is putting things in the wrong places; the worst of it is **shirk**, setting up partners with Allah.*

3. *Oppression is darkness in this worldly life, in the face of the oppressor and in his heart; it is many layers of darkness in the Hereafter.*

4. *A believer must repent from oppression and fix what he has harmed.*

5. *One of our duties as Muslim brothers is to avoid oppression in all its forms.*

الحديث الثلاثون
الظلم

عَنِ ابْنِ عُمَرَ ــ رَضِيَ اللهُ عَنْهُمَا ــ قَالَ: قَالَ رَسُولُ اللهِ ــ صَلَّى اللهُ عَلَيْهِ وَسَلَّمَ ــ :

«الظُّلْمُ ظُلُمَاتٌ يَوْمَ القِيَامَةِ.»

أَخْرَجَهُ الْبُخَارِيُّ (٢٤٤٧) وَمُسْلِمٌ (٢٥٧٩).

ما يستفاد من الحديث:

١ _ كيف تنصر أخاك الظالم؟ ذكِّره بهذا الحديث!

٢ _ الظلم وضع شيء في غير محله، وأقبحه: الشرك بالله.

٣ _ الظلم ظلمة في الدنيا في وجه الظالم وفي قلبه، وهو ظلمات في الآخرة.

٤ _ يجب على المؤمن أن يتوب من الظلم ويصلح ما أفسده.

٥ _ من واجبات الأخوة الإسلامية ترك الظلم كله.

HADEETH 31
The Rights of Muslims

Abu Hurayrah (may Allah be pleased with him) reported that the Messenger of Allah (may Allah raise his rank and grant him peace) said:

"A Muslim is a brother to another Muslim; he does not oppress him, nor does he forsake him or belittle him."

It was collected by Muslim (2564).

POINTS OF BENEFIT FROM THIS HADEETH:

1. *Oppressing any person will be layers of darkness on the Day of Judgment; oppressing your Muslim brother is even worse.*

2. *A Muslim aids his Muslim brother and does not forsake him.*

3. *A Muslim respects his Muslim brother and does not belittle him.*

4. *Islamic brotherhood is not a claim or a slogan; it is real actions in practice.*

5. *A true believer is honest and sincere with his Muslim brothers.*

الحديث الحادي والثلاثون
حقوق المسلمين

عَنْ أَبِي هُرَيْرَةَ _رَضِيَ اللهُ عَنْهُ_ قَالَ: قَالَ رَسُولُ اللهِ _صَلَّى اللهُ عَلَيْهِ وَسَلَّمَ_ :

«الْمُسْلِمُ أَخُو الْمُسْلِمِ، لَا يَظْلِمُهُ، وَلَا يَخْذُلُهُ، وَلَا يَحْقِرُهُ.»

أَخْرَجَهُ مُسْلِمٌ (٢٥٦٤).

ما يستفاد من الحديث:

١_ ظلم أحد من الناس ظلمات يوم القيامة، وظلم أخيك المسلم أشد.

٢_ المسلم يساعد أخاه المسلم ولا يخذله.

٣_ المسلم يحترم أخاه المسلم ولا يحقره.

٤_ الأخوة الإسلامية ليست مجرد دعوى أو شعار، بل هي تطبيق عملي.

٥_ المؤمن يكون صديقا مخلصا مع إخوانه المؤمنين.

HADEETH 32
Companionship

Ibn Mas'ud (may Allah be pleased with him) reported that the Messenger of Allah (may Allah raise his rank and grant him peace) said:

"A man will be with those he loves."

It was collected by al-Bukhari (6168) and Muslim (2640).

POINTS OF BENEFIT FROM THIS HADEETH:

1. *A true believer loves the believers, and the proof for his love of them is that he is with them in this world and in the Hereafter.*

2. *A disbeliever loves other disbelievers, and he is with them in this world and in the Hereafter.*

3. *Birds of a feather flock together.*

4. *Honest, trustworthy people are with people like them in this world and in the Hereafter.*

5. *Liars, hypocrites, and tricksters are with people like them in this world and in the Hereafter.*

الحديث الثاني والثلاثون
الصداقة

عَنِ ابْنِ مَسْعُودٍ ـرَضِيَ اللهُ عَنْهُ ـ قَالَ: قَالَ رَسُوْلُ اللهِ ـصَلَّى اللهُ عَلَيْهِ وَسَلَّمَ ـ :

«الْمَرْءُ مَعَ مَنْ أَحَبَّ.»

أَخْرَجَهُ الْبُخَارِيُّ (٦١٦٨) وَمُسْلِمٌ (٢٦٤٠).

ما يستفاد من الحديث:

١_ المؤمن يحب المؤمنين، ودليل محبته لهم أن يكون معهم في الدنيا والآخرة.

٢_ الكافر يحب الكافرين ويكون معهم في الدنيا والآخرة.

٣_ الطيور على أشكالها تقع.

٤_ أهل الصدق والأمانة يكونون مع أمثالهم في الدنيا والآخرة.

٥_ أهل الكذب والنفاق والخداع يكونون مع أمثالهم في الدنيا والآخرة.

HADEETH 33
Deception

Abu Hurayrah (may Allah be pleased with him) reported that the Messenger of Allah (may Allah raise his rank and grant him peace) said:

"Whoever deceives [others] is not of me."

It was collected by Muslim (102).

POINTS OF BENEFIT FROM THIS HADEETH:

1. A true believer is sincere to Allah and honest with Allah's worshippers.

2. The Prophet (may Allah raise his rank and grant him peace) freed himself of deceivers.

3. A deceiver tricks people without right, and this is a kind of oppression.

4. Deception can be in speech, during exams, or any act of worship or interaction.

5. Muslims must be warned of deceptive people.

الحديث الثالث والثلاثون
الغش

عَنْ أَبِي هُرَيْرَةَ ـرَضِيَ اللهُ عَنْهُ ـ قَالَ: قَالَ رَسُولُ اللهِ ـصَلَّى اللهُ عَلَيْهِ وَسَلَّمَ ـ:

«مَنْ غَشَّ فَلَيْسَ مِنِّي.»

أَخْرَجَهُ مُسْلِمٌ (١٠٢).

ما يستفاد من الحديث:

١ـ المؤمن مخلص لله وصادق مع عباد الله.

٢ـ تبرأ النبي صلى الله عليه وسلم من الغشاش.

٣ـ الغشاش يخدع الناس بغير حق، وهذا من الظلم.

٤ـ الغش قد يكون في الكلام، وفي الاختبارات، وفي كل العبادات والمعاملات.

٥ـ يجب أن يكون المسلمون على حذر من الغشاشين.

HADEETH 34
Being Aware of Evil

Abu Hurayrah (may Allah be pleased with him) reported that the Messenger of Allah (may Allah raise his rank and grant him peace) said:

"A true believer is not stung from the same hole twice."

It was collected by al-Bukhari (6133) and Muslim (2998).

POINTS OF BENEFIT FROM THIS HADEETH:

1. *Muslims must be aware of the plots of people of evil and deception.*

2. *A true believer is smart; he learns from his mistakes so he does not do them again.*

3. *From the bad effects of oppression is that the victims will not trust the oppressor again.*

4. *A true believer has good thoughts about honest and trustworthy people, but not liars and deceivers.*

5. *Being warned of evil does not go against Islamic brotherhood.*

الحديث الرابع والثلاثون
الحذر من الشر

عَنْ أَبِي هُرَيْرَةَ ـرَضِيَ اللهُ عَنْهُ ـ قَالَ: قَالَ رَسُولُ اللهِ ـصَلَّى اللهُ عَلَيْهِ وَسَلَّمَ ـ :

«لاَ يُلْدَغُ الْمُؤْمِنُ مِنْ جُحْرٍ وَاحِدٍ مَرَّتَيْنِ.»

أَخْرَجَهُ الْبُخَارِيُّ (٦١٣٣) وَمُسْلِمٌ (٢٩٩٨).

ما يستفاد من الحديث:

١ _ يحذر المسلمون من كيد أهل الشر والغشاشين.

٢ _ المؤمن ذكي يتعلم من أخطائه حتى لا يقع فيها مرة أخرى.

٣ _ من شر آثار الظلم أن المظلوم لا يثق بالظالم.

٤ _ المؤمن يحسن الظن بأهل الصدق والأمانة، لا بالكذابين والغشاشين.

٥ _ الحذر من الشر لا يناقض الأخوة الإسلامية.

PART SIX

FOCUSING

ON GOOD

الْبَابُ السَّادِسُ

الْحِرْصُ

عَلَى الْخَيْرِ

HADEETH 35
Good Health & Free Time

Ibn 'Abbas (may Allah be pleased with him) reported that the Messenger of Allah (may Allah raise his rank and grant him peace) said:

"Two blessings are overlooked by many people: good health and free time."

It was collected by al-Bukhari (6412).

POINTS OF BENEFIT FROM THIS HADEETH:

1. *A true believer thinks about Allah's Blessings and thanks Him for them.*
2. *A true believer uses Allah's Blessings for good; this is part of being thankful.*
3. *Good health is a great blessing; no one really knows about it like the one who lost it.*
4. *Free time is a great blessing; life is very difficult without it.*
5. *The blessings of Allah are too many to count; a true believer is focused on using them for Allah's obedience.*

الحديث الخامس والثلاثون
الصحة والفراغ

عَنِ ابْنِ عَبَّاسٍ ــرَضِيَ اللهُ عَنْهُمَا ــ قَالَ: قَالَ رَسُولُ اللهِ ــصَلَّى اللهُ عَلَيْهِ وَسَلَّمَ ــ:

«نِعْمَتَانِ مَغْبُوْنٌ فِيْهِمَا كَثِيْرٌ مِنَ النَّاسِ: الصِّحَّةُ وَالْفَرَاغُ.»

أَخْرَجَهُ الْبُخَارِيُّ (٦٤١٢).

ما يستفاد من الحديث:

١ ــ المؤمن يتفكر في نعم الله ويشكره عليها.

٢ ــ المؤمن يستعمل نعم الله في خير، وذلك من شكر النعم.

٣ ــ الصحة نعمة عظيمة، لا يعرفها حقا إلا من فقد شيئا منها.

٤ ــ الفراغ نعمة عظيمة، وبدونه تكون الحياة صعبة جدا.

٥ ــ نعم الله كثيرة لا تحصى، والمؤمن حريص على استعمالها في طاعة الله.

HADEETH 36
Focus on Benefit

Abu Hurayrah (may Allah be pleased with him) reported that the Messenger of Allah (may Allah raise his rank and grant him peace) said:

"Be focused on what benefits you, seek the help of Allah, and do not be lazy."

It was collected by Muslim (2664).

POINTS OF BENEFIT FROM THIS HADEETH:

1. *Good health and free time are beneficial, so a true believer is focused on them.*

2. *A true believer is smart; he thinks carefully about things and focuses on the most beneficial of them.*

3. *A true believer always seeks help from Allah;* **"You [alone] we worship, and You [alone] we ask for help."** *[1:4]*

4. *Being focused on beneficial things includes: learning and practicing what we learn, with sincerity, and not being lazy.*

5. *The ways to good are many, so a true believer focuses on whatever of that Allah makes easy for him.*

الحديث السادس والثلاثون
الحرص على المفيد

عَنْ أَبِي هُرَيْرَةَ ـ رَضِيَ اللهُ عَنْهُ ـ قَالَ: قَالَ رَسُولُ اللهِ ـ صَلَّى اللهُ عَلَيْهِ وَسَلَّمَ ـ:

«احْرِصْ عَلَى مَا يَنْفَعُكَ، وَاسْتَعِنْ بِاللهِ، وَلَا تَعْجَزْ.»

أَخْرَجَهُ مُسْلِمٌ (٢٦٦٤).

ما يستفاد من الحديث:

١ _ الصحة والفراغ من الأمور المفيدة، فالمؤمن يحرص عليهما.

٢ _ المؤمن ذكي يميز بين الأمور ويحرص على أنفعها.

٣ _ يستعين المؤمن بالله دائما: {إياك نعبد وإياك نستعين}.

٤ _ من الحرص على المفيد: الاهتمام بالتعلم والتطبيق بالإخلاص، وترك الكسل.

٥ _ أبواب الخير كثيرة، فيحرص المؤمن على ما ييسره الله له منها.

HADEETH 37
Many Ways of Good

Jabir (may Allah be pleased with him) reported that the Messenger of Allah (may Allah raise his rank and grant him peace) said:

"Every good thing is a charity."

It was collected by al-Bukhari (6021).

POINTS OF BENEFIT FROM THIS HADEETH:

1. *Every good thing Allah loves is rewarded as a charity by the one who did it.*

2. *A child can give charity to his own parents by being kind to them, speaking well, and by serving and helping them.*

3. *A person can give charity to his own self by praying his prayers well and being sincere to Allah.*

4. *Our Lord is generous; He made many ways for us to give in charity by doing easy things.*

5. *Giving someone a date is charity, even half of a date!*

الحديث السابع والثلاثون
أبواب الخير كثيرة

عَنْ جَابِرٍ ـرَضِيَ اللهُ عَنْهُ ـ قَالَ: قَالَ رَسُولُ اللهِ ـصَلَّى اللهُ عَلَيْهِ وَسَلَّمَ ـ :

«كُلُّ مَعْرُوْفٍ صَدَقَةٌ.»

أَخْرَجَهُ الْبُخَارِيُّ (٦٠٢١).

ما يستفاد من الحديث:

١ _ كل ما يحبه الله من الخير يكتب لمن قام به أجر صدقة.

٢ _ يتصدق الصغير على والديه بالبر والكلام الحسن وبالخدمة والمساعدة.

٣ _ يتصدق الإنسان على نفسه بأداء الصلاة بإحسان وإخلاص لله مثلا.

٤ _ ربنا كريم قد يسر لنا أجر الصدقة في أعمال يسيرة.

٥ _ في إعطاء زميلك تمرة صدقة، حتى نصف تمرة!

HADEETH 38
Charity Saves You From Hell

'Adiy ibn Hatim (may Allah be pleased with him) reported that the Messenger of Allah (may Allah raise his rank and grant him peace) said:

"Protect yourself from the Fire, even if it is with half of a date. One who does not even have that can speak a good word."

It was collected by al-Bukhari (6540) and Muslim (1016).

POINTS OF BENEFIT FROM THIS HADEETH:

1. *A poor person has no excuse for not giving charity, because every good deed is a charity.*

2. *A true believer is afraid of Allah and His punishment.*

3. *A believer's fear of the Hellfire leads him to do good deeds.*

4. *Any good deed can save a person from Allah's punishment.*

5. *Never overlook a chance to give a small gift or even just say a kind word, like reminding someone about important manners.*

الحديث الثامن والثلاثون
الصدقة تنجيك من النار

عَنْ عَدِيِّ بْنِ حَاتِمٍ ـرَضِيَ اللهُ عَنْهُـ قَالَ: قَالَ رَسُولُ اللهِ ـصَلَّى اللهُ عَلَيْهِ وَسَلَّمَـ :

«اتَّقُوا النَّارَ وَلَوْ بِشِقِّ تَمْرَةٍ، فَمَنْ لَمْ يَجِدْ فَبِكَلِمَةٍ طَيِّبَةٍ.»

أَخْرَجَهُ الْبُخَارِيُّ (٦٥٤٠) وَمُسْلِمٌ (١٠١٦).

ما يستفاد من الحديث:

١_ الفقير لا عذر له في ترك الصدقات، لأن كل معروف صدقة.

٢_ المؤمن يخاف الله ويخاف عذابه.

٣_ خوف المؤمن من النار يعينه على أعمال صالحة.

٤_ الشيء اليسير من الخير يد ينجيك من عذاب الله.

٥_ المؤمن لا تفوته الفرصة أن يعطي الهدية الصغيرة أو أن يقول الكلمة الطيبة، كأن ينصح أحدا بآداب مهمة.

HADEETH 39
Manners of Eating

'Umar ibn Abee Salamah (may Allah be pleased with him) said: I was in the house of the Messenger of Allah (may Allah raise his rank and grant him peace), and my hand was reaching all over the plate [of food], so he said to me:

"O young boy! Mention Allah's Name, eat with your right hand, and eat from what is closest to you."

It was collected by al-Bukhari (5376) and Muslim (2022).

POINTS OF BENEFIT FROM THIS HADEETH:

1. *A child should be with adults and people of knowledge and learn important manners from them.*
2. *Manners of eating are from Allah's Religion; we practice them and remind others about them.*
3. *Before eating, we say: **"Bismillaah"** (In the Name of Allah).*
4. *We eat and drink with the right hand, not the left.*
5. *We eat from the food which is closest to us.*

الحديث التاسع والثلاثون
آداب الأكل

عَنْ عُمَرَ بْنِ أَبِي سَلَمَةَ ــرَضِيَ اللهُ عَنْهُمَا ــ قَالَ: كُنْتُ فِي حِجْرِ رَسُولِ اللهِ ــصَلَّى اللهُ عَلَيْهِ وَسَلَّمَ ــ، وَكَانَتْ يَدِي تَطِيشُ فِي الصَّحْفَةِ، فَقَالَ لِي:

«يَا غُلَامُ! سَمِّ اللهَ، وَكُلْ بِيَمِينِكَ، وَكُلْ مِمَّا يَلِيكَ.»

أَخْرَجَهُ الْبُخَارِيُّ (٥٣٧٦) وَمُسْلِمٌ (٢٠٢٢).

ما يستفاد من الحديث:

١ _ الصغير يجالس الكبار وأهل العلم ويتعلم منهم الآداب المهمة.

٢ _ آداب الطعام من دين الله؛ نطبقها وندعو إليها.

٣ _ قبل الأكل نقول: بسم الله.

٤ _ نأكل ونشرب باليمين، لا بالشمال.

٥ _ نأكل من أقرب الطعام إلينا.

HADEETH 40
Anger

Abu Hurayrah (may Allah be pleased with him) reported that a man asked the Messenger of Allah (may Allah raise his rank and grant him peace) for advice, so he said:

"Do not get angry."

The man then repeated that [request] many times; each time he said:

"Do not get angry."

It was collected by al-Bukhari (6116).

POINTS OF BENEFIT FROM THIS HADEETH:

1. *A true believer is not led by emotions; he works to train himself and improve his manners.*

2. *Anger leads to many evils.*

3. *Sometimes words need repeated to stress how important they are.*

4. *A true believer asks people of knowledge for beneficial advice.*

5. *A strong believer controls himself and does not unleash his anger.*

الحديث الأربعون
الغضب

عَنْ أَبِي هُرَيْرَةَ ـرَضِيَ اللهُ عَنْهُ ـ: أَنَّ رَجُلًا قَالَ لِلنَّبِيِّ ـصَلَّى اللهُ عَلَيْهِ وَسَلَّمَ ـ: أَوْصِنِي، قَالَ:

«لاَ تَغْضَبْ».

فَرَدَّدَ مِرَارًا، قَالَ:

«لاَ تَغْضَبْ».

أَخْرَجَهُ الْبُخَارِيُّ (٦١١٦).

ما يستفاد من الحديث:

١_ المؤمن لا تقوده عواطفه، بل يهذب نفسه وأخلاقه.

٢_ الغضب يؤدي إلى شرور كثيرة.

٣_ تكرار الكلمة المهمة من أجل التوكيد على أهميتها.

٤_ المؤمن يطلب من أهل العلم الوصايا النافعة.

٥_ المؤمن القوي يملك نفسه ولا ينفذ غضبه.

HADEETH 41
The Strong Believer

Abu Hurayrah (may Allah be pleased with him) reported that the Messenger of Allah (may Allah raise his rank and grant him peace) said:

"A man is not strong because he can overpower people; a strong man is the one who controls himself when angry."

It was collected by al-Bukhari (6114) and Muslim (2609).

POINTS OF BENEFIT FROM THIS HADEETH:

1. *The last hadeeth is about preventing anger before it comes; this hadith is about managing anger after it comes.*

2. *The strength of a true believer is in his character and how well he can control himself when angry.*

3. *A weak person hits others and insults them when he gets angry.*

4. *Kindness and good character are very important manners of true believers.*

5. *One who does not control his anger says bad things and then regrets what he said later.*

الحديث الحادي والأربعون
المؤمن القوي

عَنْ أَبِي هُرَيْرَةَ ـرَضِيَ اللهُ عَنْهُ ـ قَالَ: قَالَ رَسُولُ اللهِ ـصَلَّى اللهُ عَلَيْهِ وَسَلَّمَ ـ :

«لَيْسَ الشَّدِيْدُ بِالصُّرَعَةِ؛ إِنَّمَا الشَّدِيْدُ الَّذِي يَمْلِكُ نَفْسَهُ عِنْدَ الْغَضَبِ.»

أَخْرَجَهُ الْبُخَارِيُّ (٦١١٤) وَمُسْلِمٌ (٢٦٠٩).

ما يستفاد من الحديث:

١ _ الحديث السابق قبل الغضب، وهذا الحديث في حالة الغضب.

٢ _ قوة المؤمن في أخلاقه وكيف يملك نفسه عند الغضب.

٣ _ الضعيف هو الذي يضرب الآخرين ويسبهم عند الغضب.

٤ _ الرفق وحسن الخلق من أهم صفات المؤمنين.

٥ _ الذي لا يملك نفسه عند الغضب يطلق لسانه ثم يندم كثيرا.

HADEETH 42
Silence

Abu Hurayrah (may Allah be pleased with him) reported that the Messenger of Allah (may Allah raise his rank and grant him peace) said:

"Whoever believes in Allah and the Last Day must say [only] good things or be quiet."

It was collected by al-Bukhari (6018) and Muslim (47).

POINTS OF BENEFIT FROM THIS HADEETH:

1. *Improving your manners and not talking a lot is from the Religion, especially when you are upset.*

2. *Good speech is from faith in Allah and the Last Day.*

3. *A true believer is quiet if he has nothing helpful to say.*

4. *Faith is found on a believer's tongue, and in his actions and manners.*

5. *Remembering Allah is one of the best kinds of good speech.*

الحديث الثاني والأربعون
الصمت

عَنْ أَبِي هُرَيْرَةَ ـرَضِيَ اللهُ عَنْهُ ـ قَالَ: قَالَ رَسُولُ اللهِ ـصَلَّى اللهُ عَلَيْهِ وَسَلَّمَـ:

«مَنْ كَانَ يُؤْمِنُ بِاللهِ وَالْيَوْمِ الْآخِرِ فَلْيَقُلْ خَيْرًا أَوْ لِيَصْمُتْ».

أَخْرَجَهُ الْبُخَارِيُّ (٦٠١٨) وَمُسْلِمٌ (٤٧).

ما يستفاد من الحديث:

١_ تهذيب النفس والإمساك عن كثير من الكلام من الدين، خاصة عند الغضب.

٢_ من الإيمان بالله واليوم الآخر الكلمة الطيبة.

٣_ المؤمن يسكت إذا لم يكن في كلامه مصلحة راجحة.

٤_ الإيمان يوجد على لسان المؤمن وفي أعماله وفي أخلاقه.

٥_ من أحسن الكلمات الطيبة: ذكر الله تعالى.

HADEETH 43
Two Great Words

Abu Hurayrah (may Allah be pleased with him) reported that the Messenger of Allah (may Allah raise his rank and grant him peace) said:

"There are two words which are light on the tongue, heavy in the scale, and beloved to ar-Rahman (the Most Merciful): Exalted is Allah and the praise is His; exalted is Allah, the Great One."

It was collected by al-Bukhari (6682) and Muslim (2694).

POINTS OF BENEFIT FROM THIS HADEETH:

1. *Good speech goes into the Scale on the Day of Judgment, and it will have weight.*

2. ***"Exalted is Allah"*** *means: I declare Allah free of every type of fault or defect.*

3. ***"The praise is His"*** *means: I praise Him, out of love.*

4. *Allah loves some of our speech; a true believer repeats the words which Allah loves.*

5. *Allah is generous; He gives great rewards to people who do basic actions. (Look back at Hadeeth 24.)*

الحديث الثالث والأربعون
كلمتان عظيمتان

عَنْ أَبِي هُرَيْرَةَ ـرَضِيَ اللهُ عَنْهُ ـ قَالَ: قَالَ رَسُولُ اللهِ ـصَلَّى اللهُ عَلَيْهِ وَسَلَّمَ ـ:

«كَلِمَتَانِ خَفِيفَتَانِ عَلَى اللِّسَانِ، ثَقِيلَتَانِ فِي الْمِيزَانِ، حَبِيبَتَانِ إِلَى الرَّحْمَنِ: سُبْحَانَ اللهِ وَبِحَمْدِهِ، سُبْحَانَ اللهِ الْعَظِيمِ.»

أَخْرَجَهُ الْبُخَارِيُّ (٦٦٨٢) وَمُسْلِمٌ (٢٦٩٤).

ما يستفاد من الحديث:

١ ـ الكلام الحسن يدخل الميزان يوم القيامة وله وزن.

٢ ـ «سُبْحَانَ اللهِ» يعني: أنزه الله تعالى عن كل نقص وعيب.

٣ ـ معنى «بِحَمْدِهِ»: الثناء عليه مع المحبة.

٤ ـ الله يحب بعض الكلام منا، فالمؤمن يجتهد في تكرار ما يحبه الله.

٥ ـ الله كريم حيث رتب الثواب العظيم على العمل اليسير.
[راجع: حـ٢٤]

APPENDIX I:
Forty Hadeeth for Muslim Youth & Beginners

In the Name of Allah,
the Most Gracious, the Ever Merciful

PART ONE: SINCERITY & FOLLOWING

1. 'Umar (may Allah be pleased with him) reported that the Messenger of Allah (may Allah raise his rank and grant him peace) said: **"Actions are only by the intentions, and every person will only get what he intended."** It was collected by al-Bukhari (1) and Muslim (1907).

2. Abu Hurayrah (may Allah be pleased with him) reported that the Messenger of Allah (may Allah raise his rank and grant him peace) said: **"Allah does not look at your shapes or your wealth; instead He looks at your hearts and your actions."** It was collected by Muslim (2564).

3. 'Abdullah ibn 'Amr (may Allah be pleased with him) reported that the Messenger of Allah (may Allah raise his rank and grant him peace) said**: "O Allah, Turner of the Hearts! Turn our hearts towards Your obedience!"** It was collected by Muslim (2654).

4. Abu Hurayrah (may Allah be pleased with him) reported that the Messenger of Allah (may Allah raise his rank and grant him peace) said: **"Stay away from all things I have forbidden you from; do as much as you can of what I have told you to do."** It was collected by al-Bukhari (7288) and Muslim (1337).

5. Mu'adh ibn Jabal (may Allah be pleased with him) reported that the Messenger of Allah (may Allah raise his rank and grant him peace) said: **"Allah's right over His servants is that they worship Him alone, without worshipping any partners along with Him."** It was collected by al-Bukhari (5967) and Muslim (30).

6. Anas (may Allah be pleased with him) reported that the Messenger of Allah (may Allah raise his rank and grant him peace) said: **"Make things easy [for people], and do not make things hard; give good news, and do not run [them] away."** It was collected by al-Bukhari (69) and Muslim (1734).

7. Abu Hurayrah (may Allah be pleased with him) reported that the Messenger of Allah (may Allah raise his rank and grant him peace) said: **"The Religion is easy; no one tries to make it difficult, except that it overtakes him."** It was collected by al-Bukhari (39).

8. 'A'ishah (may Allah be pleased with her) reported that the Messenger of Allah (may Allah raise his rank and grant him peace) said: **"Whoever does any action which is not in line with our affair will have it rejected."** It was collected by al-Bukhari (2697) and Muslim (1718).

PART TWO: THE BEST DEEDS

9. 'Uthman (may Allah be pleased with him) reported that the Messenger of Allah (may Allah raise his rank and grant him peace) said: **"The best of you are those who learn the Quran and teach it."** It was collected by al-Bukhari (5027).

10. Abu Malik al-Ash'ari (may Allah be pleased with him) reported that the Messenger of Allah (may Allah raise his rank and grant him peace) said: **"The Quran is a proof for you or against you."** It was collected by Muslim (223).

11. Mu'awiyah ibn Abee Sufyan (may Allah be pleased with him) reported that the Messenger of Allah (may Allah raise his rank and grant him peace) said: **"When Allah wants good for someone, He gives him Fiqh in the Religion."** It was collected by al-Bukhari (71) and Muslim (1037).

12. Sa'd ibn Abee Waqqas (may Allah be pleased with him) reported that the Messenger of Allah (may Allah raise his rank and grant him peace) said: **"Allah loves the pious, content, humble worshipper."** It was collected by Muslim (2965).

13. Ibn Mas'ud (may Allah be pleased with him) reported that the Messenger of Allah (may Allah raise his rank and grant him peace) used to say: **"O Allah! I do ask You for guidance, piety, chastity, and contentment."** It was collected by Muslim (2721).

14. Abu Hurayrah (may Allah be pleased with him) reported that the Messenger of Allah (may Allah raise his rank and grant him peace) said: **"Real contentment is the contentment of the soul."** It was collected by al-Bukhari (6446) and Muslim (1051).

15. Ibn 'Umar (may Allah be pleased with him) reported that the Messenger of Allah (may Allah raise his rank and grant him peace) grabbed his shoulder and said: **"Be in this world like a stranger or a traveler."** It was collected by al-Bukhari (6416).

16. Abu Hurayrah (may Allah be pleased with him) reported that the Messenger of Allah (may Allah raise his rank and grant him peace) said: **"Islam started as something strange, and it will return to being strange, so Toobaa to the strangers."** It was collected by Muslim (145). *"Toobaa"* means: good news.

17. Sufyan ibn 'Abdillah ath-Thaqafi (may Allah be pleased with him) said to the Prophet (may Allah raise his rank and grant him peace): O Messenger of Allah! Tell me something about Islam that I will not need to ask anyone after you? He replied: **"Say: 'I believe in Allah,' and then be upright."** It was collected by Muslim (38).

18. 'A'ishah (may Allah be pleased with her) reported that the Messenger of Allah (may Allah raise his rank and grant him peace) said: **"The most beloved deeds to Allah, the Most High, are those done consistently, even if they are not many."** It was collected by al-Bukhari (6464) and Muslim (783).

19. Ibn Mas'ud (may Allah be pleased with him) reported that the Messenger of Allah (may Allah raise his rank and grant him peace) said: **"The best deeds are prayer in its time and kindness to parents."** It was collected by al-Bukhari (7534) and Muslim (85).

PART THREE: HONESTY

20. Abu Bakrah (may Allah be pleased with him) reported that the Messenger of Allah (may Allah raise his rank and grant him peace) said: **"The worst major sins are setting up partners with Allah, bad treatment of parents, and false speech."** It was collected by al-Bukhari (6919) and Muslim (87).

21. Abu Hurayrah (may Allah be pleased with him) reported that the Messenger of Allah (may Allah raise his rank and grant him peace) said: **"The signs of a hypocrite are three: when he speaks, he lies; when he promises something, he breaks his promise; and when he is**

trusted, he betrays." It was collected by al-Bukhari (33) and Muslim (59).

22. Abu Hurayrah (may Allah be pleased with him) reported that the Messenger of Allah (may Allah raise his rank and grant him peace) said: **"Whoever lies on me intentionally will take his seat in the Hellfire."** It was collected by al-Bukhari (110) and Muslim (3).

PART FOUR: CALLING TO THE WAY OF ALLAH

23. 'Abdullah ibn 'Amr (may Allah be pleased with him) reported that the Messenger of Allah (may Allah raise his rank and grant him peace) said: **"Share from me [what I teach, to others], even if it is just one verse."** It was collected by al-Bukhari (3461).

24. Sahl ibn Sa'd (may Allah be pleased with him) reported that the Messenger of Allah (may Allah raise his rank and grant him peace) said: **"For Allah to guide just one person by way of you is better for you than having red camels."** It was collected by al-Bukhari (3701) and Muslim (2406). **"Red camels"** means the best kinds of wealth.

25. Abu Mas'ud al-Ansari (may Allah be pleased with him) reported that the Messenger of Allah (may Allah raise his rank and grant him peace) said: **"Whoever guides [others] to something good shall have a reward like the one who does it."** It was collected by Muslim (1893).

PART FIVE: ISLAMIC BROTHERHOOD

26. Anas (may Allah be pleased with him) reported that the Messenger of Allah (may Allah raise his rank and grant him peace) said: **"None of you truly believes until he loves for his brother what he loves for himself."** It was collected by al-Bukhari (13) and Muslim (45).

27. Abu Moosa (may Allah be pleased with him) reported that the Messenger of Allah (may Allah raise his rank and grant him peace) said: **"A believer with another believer is like how some parts of a building strengthen other parts."** It was collected by al-Bukhari (2446) and Muslim (2585).

28. Abu Hurayrah (may Allah be pleased with him) reported that the Messenger of Allah (may Allah raise his rank and grant him peace) said: **"Allah aids a person, so long as**

that person aids his brother." It was collected by Muslim (2699).

29. Anas (may Allah be pleased with him) reported that the Messenger of Allah (may Allah raise his rank and grant him peace) said: **"Help your brother, whether he is an oppressor or a victim."** It was collected by al-Bukhari (2443).

30. Ibn 'Umar (may Allah be pleased with him) reported that the Messenger of Allah (may Allah raise his rank and grant him peace) said: **"Oppression is many layers of darkness on the Day of Judgment."** It was collected by al-Bukhari (2447) and Muslim (2579).

31. Abu Hurayrah (may Allah be pleased with him) reported that the Messenger of Allah (may Allah raise his rank and grant him peace) said: **"A Muslim is a brother to another Muslim; he does not oppress him, nor does he forsake him or belittle him."** It was collected by Muslim (2564).

32. Ibn Mas'ud (may Allah be pleased with him) reported that the Messenger of Allah (may Allah raise his rank and grant him peace) said: **"A man will be with those he loves."** It was collected by al-Bukhari (6168) and Muslim (2640).

33. Abu Hurayrah (may Allah be pleased with him) reported that the Messenger of Allah (may Allah raise his rank and grant him peace) said: **"Whoever deceives [others] is not of me."** It was collected by Muslim (102).

34. Abu Hurayrah (may Allah be pleased with him) reported that the Messenger of Allah (may Allah raise his rank and grant him peace) said: **"A true believer is not stung from the same hole twice."** It was collected by al-Bukhari (6133) and Muslim (2998).

PART SIX: FOCUSING ON GOOD

35. Ibn 'Abbas (may Allah be pleased with him) reported that the Messenger of Allah (may Allah raise his rank and grant him peace) said: **"Two blessings are overlooked by many people: good health and free time."** It was collected by al-Bukhari (6412).

36. Abu Hurayrah (may Allah be pleased with him) reported that the Messenger of Allah (may Allah raise his rank and grant him peace) said: **"Be focused on what benefits you,**

seek the help of Allah, and do not be lazy." It was collected by Muslim (2664).

37. Jabir (may Allah be pleased with him) reported that the Messenger of Allah (may Allah raise his rank and grant him peace) said: **"Every good thing is a charity."** It was collected by al-Bukhari (6021).

38. 'Adiy ibn Hatim (may Allah be pleased with him) reported that the Messenger of Allah (may Allah raise his rank and grant him peace) said: **"Protect yourself from the Fire, even if it is with half of a date. One who does not even have that can speak a good word."** It was collected by al-Bukhari (6540) and Muslim (1016).

39. 'Umar ibn Abee Salamah (may Allah be pleased with him) said: I was in the house of the Messenger of Allah (may Allah raise his rank and grant him peace), and my hand was reaching all over the plate [of food], so he said to me: **"O young boy! Mention Allah's Name, eat with your right hand, and eat from what is closest to you."** It was collected by al-Bukhari (5376) and Muslim (2022).

40. Abu Hurayrah (may Allah be pleased with him) reported that a man asked the Messenger of Allah (may Allah raise his rank and grant him peace) for advice, so he said: **"Do not get angry."** The man then repeated that [request] many times; each time he said: **"Do not get angry."** It was collected by al-Bukhari (6116).

41. Abu Hurayrah (may Allah be pleased with him) reported that the Messenger of Allah (may Allah raise his rank and grant him peace) said: **"A man is not strong because he can overpower people; a strong man is the one who controls himself when angry."** It was collected by al-Bukhari (6114) and Muslim (2609).

42. Abu Hurayrah (may Allah be pleased with him) reported that the Messenger of Allah (may Allah raise his rank and grant him peace) said: **"Whoever believes in Allah and the Last Day must say [only] good things or be quiet."** It was collected by al-Bukhari (6018) and Muslim (47).

43. Abu Hurayrah (may Allah be pleased with him) reported that the Messenger of Allah (may Allah raise his rank and grant him peace) said: **"There are two words which are light on the tongue, heavy in the scale, and beloved to ar-Rahman (the Most Merciful): Exalted is Allah and the praise is His; exalted is Allah, the Great One."** It was collected by al-Bukhari (6682) and Muslim (2694).

٤٢ ـ وَعَنْ أَبِي هُرَيْرَةَ ـرَضِيَ اللهُ عَنْهُ ـ قَالَ: قَالَ رَسُولُ اللهِ ـصَلَّى اللهُ عَلَيْهِ وَسَلَّمَ ـ: «مَنْ كَانَ يُؤْمِنُ بِاللهِ وَالْيَوْمِ الْآخِرِ فَلْيَقُلْ خَيْرًا أَوْ لِيَصْمُتْ.» أَخْرَجَهُ الْبُخَارِيُّ (٦٠١٨) وَمُسْلِمٌ (٤٧).

٤٣ ـ وَعَنْ أَبِي هُرَيْرَةَ ـرَضِيَ اللهُ عَنْهُ ـ قَالَ: قَالَ رَسُولُ اللهِ ـصَلَّى اللهُ عَلَيْهِ وَسَلَّمَ ـ: «كَلِمَتَانِ خَفِيفَتَانِ عَلَى اللِّسَانِ، ثَقِيلَتَانِ فِي الْمِيزَانِ، حَبِيبَتَانِ إِلَى الرَّحْمَنِ: سُبْحَانَ اللهِ وَبِحَمْدِهِ، سُبْحَانَ اللهِ الْعَظِيمِ.» أَخْرَجَهُ الْبُخَارِيُّ (٦٦٨٢) وَمُسْلِمٌ (٢٦٩٤).

❋ ❋ ❋

٣٧ـ وَعَنْ جَابِرٍ ـرَضِيَ اللهُ عَنْهُـ قَالَ: قَالَ رَسُولُ اللهِ ـصَلَّى اللهُ عَلَيْهِ وَسَلَّمَـ : «كُلُّ مَعْرُوفٍ صَدَقَةٌ.» أَخْرَجَهُ الْبُخَارِيُّ (٦٠٢١).

٣٨ـ وَعَنْ عَدِيِّ بْنِ حَاتِمٍ ـرَضِيَ اللهُ عَنْهُـ قَالَ: قَالَ رَسُولُ اللهِ ـصَلَّى اللهُ عَلَيْهِ وَسَلَّمَـ : «اتَّقُوا النَّارَ وَلَوْ بِشِقِّ تَمْرَةٍ، فَمَنْ لَمْ يَجِدْ فَبِكَلِمَةٍ طَيِّبَةٍ.» أَخْرَجَهُ الْبُخَارِيُّ (٦٥٤٠) وَمُسْلِمٌ (١٠١٦).

٣٩ـ وَعَنْ عُمَرَ بْنِ أَبِي سَلَمَةَ ـرَضِيَ اللهُ عَنْهُمَاـ قَالَ: كُنْتُ فِي حِجْرِ رَسُولِ اللهِ ـصَلَّى اللهُ عَلَيْهِ وَسَلَّمَـ، وَكَانَتْ يَدِي تَطِيشُ فِي الصَّحْفَةِ، فَقَالَ لِي: «يَا غُلَامُ! سَمِّ اللهَ، وَكُلْ بِيَمِينِكَ، وَكُلْ مِمَّا يَلِيكَ.» أَخْرَجَهُ الْبُخَارِيُّ (٥٣٧٦) وَمُسْلِمٌ (٢٠٢٢).

٤٠ـ وَعَنْ أَبِي هُرَيْرَةَ ـرَضِيَ اللهُ عَنْهُـ : أَنَّ رَجُلًا قَالَ لِلنَّبِيِّ ـصَلَّى اللهُ عَلَيْهِ وَسَلَّمَـ : أَوْصِنِي، قَالَ: «لَا تَغْضَبْ.» فَرَدَّدَ مِرَارًا، قَالَ: «لَا تَغْضَبْ.» أَخْرَجَهُ الْبُخَارِيُّ (٦١١٦).

٤١ـ وَعَنْ أَبِي هُرَيْرَةَ ـرَضِيَ اللهُ عَنْهُـ قَالَ: قَالَ رَسُولُ اللهِ ـصَلَّى اللهُ عَلَيْهِ وَسَلَّمَـ : «لَيْسَ الشَّدِيدُ بِالصُّرَعَةِ؛ إِنَّمَا الشَّدِيدُ الَّذِي يَمْلِكُ نَفْسَهُ عِنْدَ الْغَضَبِ.» أَخْرَجَهُ الْبُخَارِيُّ (٦١١٤) وَمُسْلِمٌ (٢٦٠٩).

٣١ـ وَعَنْ أَبِي هُرَيْرَةَ ـرَضِيَ اللهُ عَنْهُ ـ قَالَ: قَالَ رَسُولُ اللهِ ـصَلَّى اللهُ عَلَيْهِ وَسَلَّمَ ـ: «الْمُسْلِمُ أَخُو الْمُسْلِمِ، لَا يَظْلِمُهُ، وَلَا يَخْذُلُهُ، وَلَا يَحْقِرُهُ.» أَخْرَجَهُ مُسْلِمٌ (٢٥٦٤).

٣٢ـ وَعَنِ ابْنِ مَسْعُودٍ ـرَضِيَ اللهُ عَنْهُ ـ قَالَ: قَالَ رَسُولُ اللهِ ـصَلَّى اللهُ عَلَيْهِ وَسَلَّمَ ـ: «الْمَرْءُ مَعَ مَنْ أَحَبَّ.» أَخْرَجَهُ الْبُخَارِيُّ (٦١٦٨) وَمُسْلِمٌ (٢٦٤٠).

٣٣ـ وَعَنْ أَبِي هُرَيْرَةَ ـرَضِيَ اللهُ عَنْهُ ـ قَالَ: قَالَ رَسُولُ اللهِ ـصَلَّى اللهُ عَلَيْهِ وَسَلَّمَ ـ: «مَنْ غَشَّ فَلَيْسَ مِنِّي.» أَخْرَجَهُ مُسْلِمٌ (١٠٢).

٣٤ـ وَعَنْ أَبِي هُرَيْرَةَ ـرَضِيَ اللهُ عَنْهُ ـ قَالَ: قَالَ رَسُولُ اللهِ ـصَلَّى اللهُ عَلَيْهِ وَسَلَّمَ ـ: «لَا يُلْدَغُ الْمُؤْمِنُ مِنْ جُحْرٍ وَاحِدٍ مَرَّتَيْنِ.» أَخْرَجَهُ الْبُخَارِيُّ (٦١٣٣) وَمُسْلِمٌ (٢٩٩٨).

الْبَابُ السَّادِسُ: الْحِرْصُ عَلَى الْخَيْرِ

٣٥ـ عَنِ ابْنِ عَبَّاسٍ ـرَضِيَ اللهُ عَنْهُمَا ـ قَالَ: قَالَ رَسُولُ اللهِ ـصَلَّى اللهُ عَلَيْهِ وَسَلَّمَ ـ: «نِعْمَتَانِ مَغْبُونٌ فِيهِمَا كَثِيرٌ مِنَ النَّاسِ: الصِّحَّةُ وَالْفَرَاغُ.» أَخْرَجَهُ الْبُخَارِيُّ (٦٤١٢).

٣٦ـ وَعَنْ أَبِي هُرَيْرَةَ ـرَضِيَ اللهُ عَنْهُ ـ قَالَ: قَالَ رَسُولُ اللهِ ـصَلَّى اللهُ عَلَيْهِ وَسَلَّمَ ـ: «احْرِصْ عَلَى مَا يَنْفَعُكَ، وَاسْتَعِنْ بِاللهِ، وَلَا تَعْجَزْ.» أَخْرَجَهُ مُسْلِمٌ (٢٦٦٤).

البابُ الخامِسُ: الأخوَّةُ الإسلامِيَّةُ

٢٦ـ عَنْ أَنَسٍ ـرَضِيَ اللهُ عَنْهُ ـ قَالَ: قَالَ رَسُولُ اللهِ ـصَلَّى اللهُ عَلَيْهِ وَسَلَّمَ ـ: «لَا يُؤْمِنُ أَحَدُكُمْ حَتَّى يُحِبَّ لِأَخِيهِ مَا يُحِبُّ لِنَفْسِهِ.» أَخْرَجَهُ الْبُخَارِيُّ (١٣) وَمُسْلِمٌ (٤٥).

٢٧ـ وَعَنْ أَبِي مُوسَى ـرَضِيَ اللهُ عَنْهُ ـ قَالَ: قَالَ رَسُولُ اللهِ ـصَلَّى اللهُ عَلَيْهِ وَسَلَّمَ ـ: «الْمُؤْمِنُ لِلْمُؤْمِنِ كَالْبُنْيَانِ، يَشُدُّ بَعْضُهُ بَعْضًا.» أَخْرَجَهُ الْبُخَارِيُّ (٢٤٤٦) وَمُسْلِمٌ (٢٥٨٥).

٢٨ـ وَعَنْ أَبِي هُرَيْرَةَ ـرَضِيَ اللهُ عَنْهُ ـ قَالَ: قَالَ رَسُولُ اللهِ ـصَلَّى اللهُ عَلَيْهِ وَسَلَّمَ ـ: «اللهُ فِي عَوْنِ الْعَبْدِ مَا كَانَ الْعَبْدُ فِي عَوْنِ أَخِيهِ.» أَخْرَجَهُ مُسْلِمٌ (٢٦٩٩).

٢٩ـ وَعَنْ أَنَسٍ ـرَضِيَ اللهُ عَنْهُ ـ قَالَ: قَالَ رَسُولُ اللهِ ـصَلَّى اللهُ عَلَيْهِ وَسَلَّمَ ـ: «انْصُرْ أَخَاكَ ظَالِمًا أَوْ مَظْلُومًا.» أَخْرَجَهُ الْبُخَارِيُّ (٢٤٤٣).

٣٠ـ وَعَنِ ابْنِ عُمَرَ ـرَضِيَ اللهُ عَنْهُمَا ـ قَالَ: قَالَ رَسُولُ اللهِ ـصَلَّى اللهُ عَلَيْهِ وَسَلَّمَ ـ: «الظُّلْمُ ظُلُمَاتٌ يَوْمَ الْقِيَامَةِ.» أَخْرَجَهُ الْبُخَارِيُّ (٢٤٤٧) وَمُسْلِمٌ (٢٥٧٩).

٢١ـ وَعَنْ أَبِي هُرَيْرَةَ ـرَضِيَ اللهُ عَنْهُ ـ قَالَ: قَالَ رَسُولُ اللهِ ـصَلَّى اللهُ عَلَيْهِ وَسَلَّمَ ـ : «آيَةُ الْمُنَافِقِ ثَلَاثٌ: إِذَا حَدَّثَ كَذَبَ، وَإِذَا وَعَدَ أَخْلَفَ، وَإِذَا اؤْتُمِنَ خَانَ.» أَخْرَجَهُ الْبُخَارِيُّ (٣٣) وَمُسْلِمٌ (٥٩).

٢٢ـ وَعَنْ أَبِي هُرَيْرَةَ ـرَضِيَ اللهُ عَنْهُ ـ قَالَ: قَالَ رَسُولُ اللهِ ـصَلَّى اللهُ عَلَيْهِ وَسَلَّمَ ـ : «مَنْ كَذَبَ عَلَيَّ مُتَعَمِّدًا فَلْيَتَبَوَّأْ مَقْعَدَهُ مِنَ النَّارِ.» أَخْرَجَهُ الْبُخَارِيُّ (١١٠) وَمُسْلِمٌ (٣).

البَابُ الرَّابِعُ: الدَّعْوَةُ إِلَى اللهِ

٢٣ـ عَنْ عَبْدِ اللهِ بْنِ عَمْرٍو ـرَضِيَ اللهُ عَنْهُمَا ـ قَالَ: قَالَ رَسُولُ اللهِ ـصَلَّى اللهُ عَلَيْهِ وَسَلَّمَ ـ : «بَلِّغُوا عَنِّي، وَلَوْ آيَةً.» أَخْرَجَهُ الْبُخَارِيُّ (٣٤٦١).

٢٤ـ وَعَنْ سَهْلِ بْنِ سَعْدٍ ـرَضِيَ اللهُ عَنْهُمَا ـ قَالَ: قَالَ رَسُولُ اللهِ ـصَلَّى اللهُ عَلَيْهِ وَسَلَّمَ ـ : «لَأَنْ يَهْدِيَ اللهُ بِكَ رَجُلًا وَاحِدًا خَيْرٌ لَكَ مِنْ أَنْ يَكُونَ لَكَ حُمْرُ النَّعَمِ.» أَخْرَجَهُ الْبُخَارِيُّ (٣٧٠١) وَمُسْلِمٌ (٢٤٠٦).

٢٥ـ وَعَنْ أَبِي مَسْعُودٍ الْأَنْصَارِيِّ ـرَضِيَ اللهُ عَنْهُ ، قَالَ: قَالَ رَسُولُ اللهِ ـصَلَّى اللهُ عَلَيْهِ وَسَلَّمَ ـ : «مَنْ دَلَّ عَلَى خَيْرٍ فَلَهُ مِثْلُ أَجْرِ فَاعِلِهِ.» أَخْرَجَهُ مُسْلِمٌ (١٨٩٣).

١٦_ وَعَنْ أَبِي هُرَيْرَةَ _رَضِيَ اللهُ عَنْهُ_ قَالَ: قَالَ رَسُولُ اللهِ _صَلَّى اللهُ عَلَيْهِ وَسَلَّمَ_ : «بَدَأَ الْإِسْلَامُ غَرِيبًا، وَسَيَعُودُ كَمَا بَدَأَ غَرِيبًا، فَطُوبَى لِلْغُرَبَاءِ.» أَخْرَجَهُ مُسْلِمٌ (١٤٥). وَمَعْنَى «طُوبَى»: بُشْرَى.

١٧_ وَعَنْ سُفْيَانَ بْنِ عَبْدِ اللهِ الثَّقَفِيِّ _رَضِيَ اللهُ عَنْهُ_ قَالَ: قُلْتُ: يَا رَسُولَ اللهِ! قُلْ لِي فِي الْإِسْلَامِ قَوْلًا لَا أَسْأَلُ عَنْهُ أَحَدًا بَعْدَكَ؟ قَالَ: «قُلْ: آمَنْتُ بِاللهِ، فَاسْتَقِمْ.» أَخْرَجَهُ مُسْلِمٌ (٣٨).

١٨_ وَعَنْ عَائِشَةَ _رَضِيَ اللهُ عَنْهَا_ قَالَتْ: قَالَ رَسُولُ اللهِ _صَلَّى اللهُ عَلَيْهِ وَسَلَّمَ_ : «أَحَبُّ الْأَعْمَالِ إِلَى اللهِ تَعَالَى أَدْوَمُهَا وَإِنْ قَلَّ.» أَخْرَجَهُ الْبُخَارِيُّ (٦٤٦٤) وَمُسْلِمٌ (٧٨٣)، وَاللَّفْظُ لَهُ.

١٩_ وَعَنِ ابْنِ مَسْعُودٍ _رَضِيَ اللهُ عَنْهُ_ قَالَ: قَالَ رَسُولُ اللهِ _صَلَّى اللهُ عَلَيْهِ وَسَلَّمَ_ : «أَفْضَلُ الْأَعْمَالِ الصَّلَاةُ لِوَقْتِهَا، وَبِرُّ الْوَالِدَيْنِ.» أَخْرَجَهُ الْبُخَارِيُّ (٧٥٣٤) وَمُسْلِمٌ (٨٥)، وَاللَّفْظُ لَهُ.

البَابُ الثَّالِثُ: الصِّدْقُ

٢٠_ عَنْ أَبِي بَكْرَةَ _رَضِيَ اللهُ عَنْهُ_ قَالَ: قَالَ رَسُولُ اللهِ _صَلَّى اللهُ عَلَيْهِ وَسَلَّمَ_ : «أَكْبَرُ الْكَبَائِرِ: الْإِشْرَاكُ بِاللهِ، وَعُقُوقُ الْوَالِدَيْنِ، وَشَهَادَةُ الزُّورِ.» أَخْرَجَهُ الْبُخَارِيُّ (٦٩١٩) وَمُسْلِمٌ (٨٧)، وَهَذَا لَفْظُ الْبُخَارِيِّ.

١٠ـ وَعَنْ أَبِي مَالِكٍ الْأَشْعَرِيّ ـرَضِيَ اللهُ عَنْهُ ـ قَالَ: قَالَ رَسُولُ اللهِ ـصَلَّى اللهُ عَلَيْهِ وَسَلَّمَ ـ : «الْقُرْآنُ حُجَّةٌ لَكَ أَوْ عَلَيْكَ.» أَخْرَجَهُ مُسْلِمٌ (٢٢٣).

١١ـ وَعَنْ مُعَاوِيَةَ بْنِ أَبِي سُفْيَانَ ـرَضِيَ اللهُ عَنْهُ ـ قَالَ: قَالَ رَسُولُ اللهِ ـ صَلَّى اللهُ عَلَيْهِ وَسَلَّمَ ـ : «مَنْ يُرِدِ اللهُ بِهِ خَيْرًا يُفَقِّهْهُ فِي الدِّينِ.» أَخْرَجَهُ الْبُخَارِيُّ (٧١) وَمُسْلِمٌ (١٠٣٧).

١٢ـ وَعَنْ سَعْدِ بْنِ أَبِي وَقَّاصٍ ـرَضِيَ اللهُ عَنْهُ ـ قَالَ: قَالَ رَسُولُ اللهِ ـصَلَّى اللهُ عَلَيْهِ وَسَلَّمَ ـ : «إِنَّ اللهَ يُحِبُّ الْعَبْدَ التَّقِيَّ الْغَنِيَّ الْخَفِيَّ.» أَخْرَجَهُ مُسْلِمٌ (٢٩٦٥).

١٣ـ وَعَنِ ابْنِ مَسْعُودٍ ـرَضِيَ اللهُ عَنْهُ ـ: عَنِ النَّبِيِّ ـصَلَّى اللهُ عَلَيْهِ وَسَلَّمَ ـ، أَنَّهُ كَانَ يَقُولُ: «اللَّهُمَّ إِنِّي أَسْأَلُكَ الْهُدَى وَالتُّقَى وَالْعَفَافَ وَالْغِنَى.» أَخْرَجَهُ مُسْلِمٌ (٢٧٢١).

١٤ـ وَعَنْ أَبِي هُرَيْرَةَ ـرَضِيَ اللهُ عَنْهُ ـ قَالَ: قَالَ رَسُولُ اللهِ ـصَلَّى اللهُ عَلَيْهِ وَسَلَّمَ ـ : «الْغِنَى غِنَى النَّفْسِ.» أَخْرَجَهُ الْبُخَارِيُّ (٦٤٤٦) وَمُسْلِمٌ (١٠٥١).

١٥ـ وَعَنِ ابْنِ عُمَرَ ـرَضِيَ اللهُ عَنْهُمَا ـ قَالَ: أَخَذَ رَسُولُ اللهِ ـصَلَّى اللهُ عَلَيْهِ وَسَلَّمَ ـ بِمَنْكِبِي، فَقَالَ: «كُنْ فِي الدُّنْيَا كَأَنَّكَ غَرِيبٌ أَوْ عَابِرُ سَبِيلٍ.» أَخْرَجَهُ الْبُخَارِيُّ (٦٤١٦).

٥ـ وَعَنْ مُعَاذِ بْنِ جَبَلٍ ـرَضِيَ اللهُ عَنْهُـ، قَالَ: قَالَ رَسُولُ اللهِ ـصَلَّى اللهُ عَلَيْهِ وَسَلَّمَـ: «حَقُّ اللهِ عَلَى عِبَادِهِ أَنْ يَعْبُدُوهُ وَلاَ يُشْرِكُوا بِهِ شَيْئًا.» أَخْرَجَهُ الْبُخَارِيُّ (٥٩٦٧) وَمُسْلِمٌ (٣٠).

٦ـ وَعَنْ أَنَسٍ ـرَضِيَ اللهُ عَنْهُـ قَالَ: قَالَ رَسُولُ اللهِ ـصَلَّى اللهُ عَلَيْهِ وَسَلَّمَـ: «يَسِّرُوا وَلاَ تُعَسِّرُوا، وَبَشِّرُوا وَلاَ تُنَفِّرُوا.» أَخْرَجَهُ الْبُخَارِيُّ (٦٩) وَمُسْلِمٌ (١٧٣٤).

٧ـ وَعَنْ أَبِي هُرَيْرَةَ ـرَضِيَ اللهُ عَنْهُـ قَالَ: قَالَ رَسُولُ اللهِ ـصَلَّى اللهُ عَلَيْهِ وَسَلَّمَـ: «إِنَّ الدِّينَ يُسْرٌ، وَلَنْ يُشَادَّ الدِّينَ أَحَدٌ إِلَّا غَلَبَهُ.» أَخْرَجَهُ الْبُخَارِيُّ (٣٩).

٨ـ وَعَنْ عَائِشَةَ ـرَضِيَ اللهُ عَنْهَاـ قَالَتْ: قَالَ رَسُولُ اللهِ ـصَلَّى اللهُ عَلَيْهِ وَسَلَّمَـ: «مَنْ عَمِلَ عَمَلًا لَيْسَ عَلَيْهِ أَمْرُنَا فَهُوَ رَدٌّ.» أَخْرَجَهُ الْبُخَارِيُّ (٢٦٩٧) وَمُسْلِمٌ (١٧١٨)، وَاللَّفْظُ لَهُ.

البَابُ الثَّانِي: أَفْضَلُ الأَعْمَالِ

٩ـ عَنْ عُثْمَانَ ـرَضِيَ اللهُ عَنْهُـ قَالَ: قَالَ رَسُولُ اللهِ ـصَلَّى اللهُ عَلَيْهِ وَسَلَّمَـ: «خَيْرُكُمْ مَنْ تَعَلَّمَ القُرْآنَ وَعَلَّمَهُ.» أَخْرَجَهُ الْبُخَارِيُّ (٥٠٢٧).

كِتابُ الأَرْبَعِينَ القِصَارِ لِلْمُتَعَلِّمِينَ الصِغارِ

بِسْمِ اللهِ الرَّحْمَنِ الرَّحِيمِ

البابُ الأَوَّلُ: الإِخْلاصُ والمُتابَعَة

١ ــ عَنْ عُمَرَ ــ رَضِيَ اللهُ عَنْهُ ــ قَالَ: قَالَ رَسُولُ اللهِ ــ صَلَّى اللهُ عَلَيْهِ وَسَلَّمَ ــ : «إِنَّمَا الأَعْمَالُ بِالنِّيَّاتِ، وَإِنَّمَا لِكُلِّ امْرِئٍ مَا نَوَى.» أَخْرَجَهُ الْبُخَارِيُّ (١) وَمُسْلِمٌ (١٩٠٧).

٢ ــ وَعَنْ أَبِي هُرَيْرَةَ ــ رَضِيَ اللهُ عَنْهُ ــ قَالَ: قَالَ رَسُولُ اللهِ ــ صَلَّى اللهُ عَلَيْهِ وَسَلَّمَ ــ : «إِنَّ اللهَ لَا يَنْظُرُ إِلَى صُوَرِكُمْ وَأَمْوَالِكُمْ، وَلكِنْ يَنْظُرُ إِلَى قُلُوبِكُمْ وَأَعْمَالِكُمْ.» أَخْرَجَهُ مُسْلِمٌ (٢٥٦٤).

٣ ــ وَعَنْ عَبْدِاللهِ بْنِ عَمْرٍو ــ رَضِيَ اللهُ عَنْهُمَا ــ قَالَ: قَالَ رَسُولُ اللهِ ــ صَلَّى اللهُ عَلَيْهِ وَسَلَّمَ ــ : «اللَّهُمَّ مُصَرِّفَ الْقُلُوبِ! صَرِّفْ قُلُوبَنَا عَلَى طَاعَتِكَ!» أَخْرَجَهُ مُسْلِمٌ (٢٦٥٤).

٤ ــ وَعَنْ أَبِي هُرَيْرَةَ ــ رَضِيَ اللهُ عَنْهُ ــ قَالَ: قَالَ رَسُولُ اللهِ ــ صَلَّى اللهُ عَلَيْهِ وَسَلَّمَ ــ : «مَا نَهَيْتُكُمْ عَنْهُ فَاجْتَنِبُوهُ، وَمَا أَمَرْتُكُمْ بِهِ فَافْعَلُوا مِنْهُ مَا اسْتَطَعْتُمْ.» أَخْرَجَهُ الْبُخَارِيُّ (٧٢٨٨) وَمُسْلِمٌ (١٣٣٧)، وَاللَّفْظُ لَهُ.

Printed in Great Britain
by Amazon

36567964R10071